THE BOY LIFE OF NAPOLEON

Afterwards Emperor Of The French

Adapted And Extended For American Boys And Girls From The French Of

Madame Eugenie Foa

The Boy Life of Napoleon

Madame Eugenie Foa

© 1st World Library – Literary Society, 2005
PO Box 2211
Fairfield, IA 52556
www.1stworldlibrary.org
First Edition

LCCN: 2004195614

Softcover ISBN: 1-4218-0435-2
Hardcover ISBN: 1-4218-0335-6
eBook ISBN: 1-4218-0535-9

Purchase *"The Boy Life of Napoleon"*
as a traditional bound book at:
www.1stWorldLibrary.org/purchase.asp?ISBN=1-4218-0435-2

1st World Library Literary Society is a nonprofit organization dedicated to promoting literacy by:

- Creating a free internet library accessible from any computer worldwide.
- Hosting writing competitions and offering book publishing scholarships.

**Readers interested in supporting literacy through sponsorship, donations or membership please contact:
literacy@1stworldlibrary.org
Check us out at: www.1stworldlibrary.ORG
and start downloading free ebooks today.**

The Boy Life of Napoleon
contributed by Tim, Ed & Rodney
in support of
1st World Library Literary Society

CONTENTS

PREFACE 9

CHAPTER ONE 10
In Napoleon's Grotto

CHAPTER TWO 23
The Canon's Pears

CHAPTER THREE 33
The Accusation

CHAPTER FOUR 40
Bread and Water

CHAPTER FIVE 49
A Wrong Righted

CHAPTER SIX 56
The Battle with the Shepherd Boys

CHAPTER SEVEN 62
Good-bye to Corsica

CHAPTER EIGHT 67
At the Preparatory School

CHAPTER NINE 72
The Lonely School-Boy

CHAPTER TEN 77
In Napoleon's Garden

CHAPTER ELEVEN 83
Friends and Foes

CHAPTER TWELVE 91
The Great Snow-tall Fight at Brienne School

CHAPTER THIRTEEN 100
Recommended for Promotion

CHAPTER FOURTEEN 108
Napoleon goes to Parts

CHAPTER FIFTEEN 115
A Trouble over Pocket Money

CHAPTER SIXTEEN 126
Lieutenant Puss-in-Boots

CHAPTER SEVENTEEN 134
Dark Days

CHAPTER EIGHTEEN 143
By the Wall of the Soldiers' Home

CHAPTER NINETEEN 152
The Little Corporal

CHAPTER TWENTY 160
"Long Live the Emperor!"

PREFACE.

The name of Madame Eugenie Foa has been a familiar one in French homes for more than a generation. Forty years ago she was the most popular writer of historical stories and sketches, especially designed for the boys and girls of France. Her tone is pure, her morals are high, her teachings are direct and effective. She has, besides, historical accuracy and dramatic action; and her twenty books for children have found welcome and entrance into the most exclusive of French homes. The publishers of this American adaptation take pleasure in introducing Madame Foa's work to American boys and girls, and in this Napoleonic renaissance are particularly favored in being able to reproduce her excellent story of the boy Napoleon.

The French original has been adapted and enlarged in the light of recent research, and all possible sources have been drawn upon to make a complete and rounded story of Napoleon's boyhood upon the basis furnished by Madame Foa's sketch. If this glimpse of the boy Napoleon shall lead young readers to the study of the later career of this marvellous man, unbiased by partisanship, and swayed neither by hatred nor hero worship, the publishers will feel that this presentation of the opening chapters of his life will not have been in vain.

CHAPTER ONE.

IN NAPOLEON'S GROTTO.

On a certain August day, in the year 1776, two little girls were strolling hand in hand along the pleasant promenade that leads from the queer little town of Ajaccio out into the open country.

The town of Ajaccio is on the western side of the beautiful island of Corsica, in the Mediterranean Sea. Back of it rise the great mountains, white with snowy tops; below it sparkles the Mediterranean, bluest of blue water. There are trees everywhere; there are flowers all about; the air is fragrant with the odor of fruit and foliage; and it was through this scented air, and amid these beautiful flowers, that these two little girls were wandering idly, picking here and there to add to their big bouquets, that August day so many years ago.

Every now and then the little girls would stop their flower-picking to cool off; for, though the August sun was hot, the western breezes came fresh across the wide Gulf of Ajaccio, down to whose shores ran broad and beautiful avenues of chestnut-trees, through which one could catch a glimpse, like a beautiful picture, of the little island of Sanguinarie, three miles away from shore.

As they came out from the shadow of the chestnut-trees, one of the little girls suddenly caught her companion's arm, and, pointing at an opening in a pile of rocks that overlooked the sea, she said, -

"Oh, what is this, Eliza? - an oven?"

"An oven, silly! Why, what do you mean?" Eliza answered. "Who would build an oven here, tell me?"

"But it opens like an oven," her friend declared. "See, it has a great mouth, as if to swallow one. Perhaps some of the black elves live there, that Nurse Camilla told us of. Do you think so, Eliza?"

"What a baby you are, Panoria!" Eliza replied, with the superior air of one who knows all about things. "That is no oven; nor is it a black elf's house. It is Napoleon's grotto."

"Napoleon's!" cried Panoria. "And who gave it to him, then? Your great uncle, the Canon Lucien?"

"No one gave it to him, child," Eliza replied. "Napoleon found it in the rocks, and teased Uncle Joey Fesch to fix it up for him. Uncle Joey did so, and Napoleon comes here so often now that we call it Napoleon's grotto."

"Does he come here all alone?" asked Panoria.

"Alone? Of course," answered Eliza. "Why should he not? He is big enough."

"No; I mean does he not let any of you come here with him?"

"That he will not!" replied Eliza. "Napoleon is such an odd boy! He will have no one but Uncle Joey Fesch come into his grotto, and that is only when he wishes Uncle Joey to teach him the primer. Brother Joseph tried to come in here one day, and Napoleon beat him and bit him, until Joseph was glad to run out, and has never since gone into the grotto."

"What if we should go in there, Eliza?" queried Panoria.

"Oh, never think of it!" cried Eliza. "Napoleon would never forgive us, and his nails are sharp."

"And what does he do in his grotto?" asked the inquisitive Panoria.

"Oh, he talks to himself," Eliza replied.

"My! but that is foolish," cried Panoria; "and stupid too."

"Then, so are you to say so," Eliza retorted. "I tell you what is true. My brother Napoleon comes here every day. He stays in his grotto for hours. He talks to himself. I know what I am saying for I have come here lots and lots of times just to listen. But I do not let him see me, or he would drive me away."

"Is he in there now?" inquired Panoria with curiosity.

"I suppose so; he always is," replied Eliza.

"Let us hide and listen, then," suggested Panoria. "I should like to know what he can say when he talks to himself. Boys are bad enough, anyway; but a boy who just talks to himself must be crazy."

Eliza was hardly ready to agree to her little friend's theory, so she said, "Wait here, Panoria, and I will go and peep into the grotto to see if Napoleon is there."

"Yes, do so," assented Panoria; "and I will run down to that garden and pick more flowers. See, there are many there."

"Oh, no, you must not," Eliza objected; "that is my uncle the Canon Lucien's garden."

"Well, and is your uncle the canon's garden more sacred than any one else's garden?" questioned Panoria flippantly.

"What a goosie you are to ask that! Of course it is," declared Eliza.

"But why?" Panoria persisted.

"Why?" echoed Eliza; "just because it is. It is the garden of my great uncle the Canon Lucien; that is why."

"It is, because it is! That is nothing," Panoria protested. "If I could not give a better reason" - "It is not my reason, Panoria," Eliza broke in. "It is Mamma Letitia's; therefore it must be right."

"Well, I don't care," Panoria declared; "even if it is your mamma's, it is - but how is it your mamma's?" she asked, changing protest to inquiry.

"Why, we hear it whenever we do anything," replied

Eliza. "If they wish to stop our play, they say, 'Stop! you will give your uncle the headache.' If we handle anything we should not, they say, 'Hands off! that belongs to your uncle the canon.' If we ask for a peach, they tell us, 'No! it is from the garden of your uncle the canon.' If they give us a hug or a kiss, when we have done well, they say, 'Oh, your uncle the canon will be so pleased with you!' Was I not right? Is not our uncle the canon beyond all others?"

"Yes; to worry one," declared Panoria rebelliously. "But why? Is it because he is canon of the cathedral here at Ajaccio that they are all so afraid of him?"

"Afraid of him!" exclaimed Eliza indignantly. "Who is afraid of him? We are not. But, you see, Papa Charles is not rich enough to do for us what he would like. If he could but have the great estates in this island which are his by right, he would be rich enough to do everything for us. But some bad people have taken the land; and even though Papa Charles is a count, he is not rich enough to send us all to school; so our uncle, the Canon Lucien, teaches us many lessons. He is not cross, let me tell you, Panoria; but he is - well, a little severe."

"What, then, does he whip you?" asked Panoria.

"No, he does not; but if he says we should be whipped, then Mamma Letitia hands us over to Nurse Mina Saveria; and she, I promise you, does not let us off from the whipping."

All this Eliza admitted as if with vivid recollections of the vigor of Nurse Saveria's arm.

Panoria glanced toward the grotto amid the rocks.

"Does he - Napoleon - ever get whipped?" she asked.

"Indeed he does not," Eliza grumbled; "or not as often as the rest of us," she added. "And when he is whipped he does not even cry. You should hear Joseph, though. Joseph is the boy to cry; and so is Lucien. I'd be ashamed to cry as they do. Why, if you touch those boys just with your little finger, they go running to Mamma Letitia, crying that we've scratched the skin off."

Panoria had her idea of such "cry-babies" of boys; but Napoleon interested her most.

"But, Eliza," she said, "what does he say - Napoleon - when he talks to himself in his grotto over there?"

"You shall hear," Eliza replied. "Let me go and peep in, to see if he is there. But no; hush! See, here he comes! Come; we will hide behind the lilac-bush, and hear what Napoleon says."

"But will not your nurse, Saveria, come to look for us?" asked Panoria, who had not forgotten Eliza's reference to the nurse's heavy hand.

"Why, no; Saveria will be busy for an hour yet, picking fruit for our table from my uncle the canon's garden. We have time," Eliza explained.

So the two little girls hid themselves behind the lilac-bushes that grew beside the rocks in which was the little cave which they called Napoleon's grotto. The bush concealed them from view; two pairs of wide-open black eyes peering curiously between the lilac-leaves were the only signs of the mischievous young eavesdroppers.

The boy who was walking thoughtfully toward the grotto did not notice the little girls. He was about seven years old. In fact, he was seven that very day. For he was born in the big, bare house in Ajaccio, which was his home, on the fifteenth of August, 1776.

He was an odd-looking boy. He was almost elf-like in appearance. His head was big, his body small, his arms and legs were thin and spindling. His long, dark hair fell about his face; his dress was careless and disordered; his stockings had tumbled down over his shoes, and he looked much like an untidy boy. But one scarcely noticed the dress of this boy. It was his face that held the attention.

It was an Italian face; for this boy's ancestors had come, not so many generations before, from the Tuscan town of Sarzana, on the Gulf of Genoa - the very town from which "the brave Lord of Luna," of whom you may read in Macaulay's splendid poem of "Horatius," came to the sack of Rome. Save for his odd appearance, with his big head and his little body, there was nothing to particularly distinguish the boy Napoleon Bonaparte from other children of his own age.

Now and then, indeed, his face would show all the shifting emotions of ambition, passion, and determination; and his eyes, though not beautiful, had in them a piercing and commanding gleam that, with a glance, could influence and attract his companions.

Whatever happened, these wonderful eyes - even in the boy - never lost the power of control which they gave to their owner over those about him. With a look through those eyes, Napoleon would appear to conceal his own thoughts and learn those of others. They could flash in anger if need be, or smile in approval; but, before their fixed and piercing glance, even the boldest and most inquisitive of other eyes lowered their lids.

Of course this eye-power, as we might call it, grew as the boy grew; but even as a little fellow in his Corsican home, this attraction asserted itself, as many a playfellow and foeman could testify, from Joey Fesch, his boy-uncle, to whom he was much attached, to Joseph his older brother, with whom he was always quarrelling, and Giacommetta, the little black-eyed girl, about whom the boys of Ajaccio teased him.

The little girls behind the lilac-bush watched the boy curiously.

"Why does he walk like that?" asked Panoria, as she noted Napoleon's advance. He came slowly, his eyes fixed on the sea, his hands clasped behind his back.

"Our uncle the canon," whispered Eliza; "he walks just that way, and Napoleon copies him."

"My, he looks about fifty!" said Panoria. "What do you suppose he is thinking about?"

"Not about us, be sure," Eliza declared.

"I believe he's dreaming," said mischievous Panoria; "let us scream out, and see if we can frighten him."

"Silly! you can't frighten Napoleon," Eliza asserted, clapping a hand over her companion's mouth. "But he could frighten you. I have tried it."

Napoleon stood a moment looking seaward, and tossed back his long hair, as if to bathe his forehead in the cooling breezes. Then entering the grotto, he flung himself on its rocky floor, and, leaning his head upon his hand, seemed as lost in meditation as any gray old hermit of the hills, all unconscious of the four black eyes which, filled with curiosity and fun, were watching him from behind the lilac-bush.

"Here, at least," the boy said, speaking aloud, as if he wished the broad sea to share his thoughts, "here I am master, here I am alone; here no one can command or control me. I am seven years old to-day. One is not a man at seven; that I know. But neither is one a child when he has my desires. Our uncle, the Canon Lucien, tells me that Spartan boys were taken away from the women when they were seven years old, and trained by men. I wish I were a Spartan. There are too many here to say what I may and may not do, - Mamma Letitia, our uncle the canon, Papa Charles, Nurse Saveria, Nurse Camilla, to say nothing of my boy-uncle Fesch, my brother Joseph, and sister Eliza; Uncle Joey Fesch is but four years older than I, my brother Joseph is but a year older, and Eliza is a year younger! Even little Pauline has her word to put in against me. Bah! why should they? If now I were but the master at home, as I am here" -

"Well, hermit! and what if you were the master?" cried Eliza from the lilac-bush.

The two girls had kept silence as long as they could;

and now, to keep Panoria from speaking out, Eliza had interrupted with her question.

With that, they both ran into the grotto.

Napoleon was silent a moment, as if protesting against this invasion of his privacy. Then he said, - "If I were the master, Eliza, I would make you both do penance for listening at doors;" for it especially mortified this boy to be overheard talking to himself.

"But here are no doors, Napoleon!" cried Eliza, whirling about in the grotto.

"So much the worse, then," Napoleon returned hotly. "When there are no doors, one should be even more careful about intruding."

"Pho! hear the little lord," teased Eliza. "One would think he was the Emperor what's his name, or the Grand Turk."

Napoleon was about to respond still more sharply, when just then a shrill voice rang through the grotto.

"Eliza; Panoria! Panoria; Eliza!" the call came. "Where are you, runaways? Where are you hidden?"

"Here we are, Saveria," Eliza cried in reply, but making no move to retire.

Napoleon would have put the girls out, but the next moment a tall and stout young woman appeared at the entrance of the grotto. She was dressed in black, with a black shawl draped over her high hair, and held by a silver pin. On her arm she carried a large basket filled with fine fruit, - pears, grapes, and figs. "So here you are, in Napoleon's grotto!" exclaimed Saveria the nurse, dropping with her basket on the ground. "Why did you run from me, naughty ones?"

Napoleon noted the basket's luscious contents.

"Oh, a pear! Give me a pear, Saveria!" he cried, springing toward the nurse, and thrusting a hand into the basket.

But Nurse Saveria hastily drew away the basket.

"Why, child, child! what are you doing?" she exclaimed. "These are your uncle the canon's."

Napoleon withdrew his hand as sharply as if a bee amid the fruit had stung him.

"Ah, is it so?" he cried; but Panoria, not having before her eyes the fear of the Bonapartes' bugbear, "their uncle the canon," laughed loudly.

"What funny people you all are!" she exclaimed. "One needs but to cry, 'Your uncle the canon,' and down you all tumble like a house of cards. What! is Saveria, too, afraid of him?"

"No more than I am," said Napoleon stoutly.

"No more than you!" laughed Panoria. "Why, Napoleon, you did not dare to even touch the pears of your uncle the canon."

"Because I did not wish to, Panoria," replied Napoleon.

Eugenie Foa

"Did not dare to," corrected Panoria.

"Did not wish to," insisted Napoleon.

"Well, wish it! I dare you to wish it!" cried Panoria, while Eliza looked on horrified at her little friend's suggestion.

By this time Saveria had led the children from the grotto, and, walking on ahead, was returning toward their home. She did not hear Panoria's "dare."

"You may dare me," Napoleon replied to the challenge of Panoria; "but if I do not wish it, you gain nothing by daring me."

"Ho! you are afraid, little boy!" cried Panoria.

"I afraid?" and Napoleon turned his piercing glance upon the little girl, so that she quailed before it.

But Panoria was an obstinate child, and she returned to the charge.

"But if you did wish it, would you do it, Napoleon?" she asked. "Of course," the boy replied.

"Oh, it is easy to brag," said Panoria; "but when your great man, your uncle the canon, is around, you are no braver, I'll be bound, than little Pauline, or even Eliza here."

By this time Eliza, too, had grown brave; and she said stoutly to her friend, "What! I am not brave, you say? You shall see."

Then as Saveria, turning, bade them hurry on, Eliza caught Panoria's hand, and ran toward the nurse; but as she did so, she said to Panoria, boastingly and rashly, -

"Come into our house! If I do not eat some of those very pears out of that very basket of our uncle the canon's, then you may call me a coward, Panoria!"

"Would you then dare?" cried Panoria. "I'll not believe it unless I see you."

Eliza was "in for it" now. "Then you shall see me!" she declared. "Come to my house. Mamma Letitia is away visiting, and I shall have the best chance. I promise you; you shall see."

"Hurry, then," said Panoria. "It is better than braving the black elves, this that you are to do, Eliza. For truly I think your uncle the canon must be an ogre."

"You shall see," Eliza declared again; and, running after Nurse Saveria, they were soon in the narrow street in which, standing across the way from a little park, was the big, bare, yellowish-gray, four-story house in which lived the Bonaparte family, always hard pushed for money, and having but few of the fine things which so large a house seemed to call for. Indeed, they would have had scarcely anything to live on had it not been for this same important relative, "our uncle, the Canon Lucien," who spent much of his yearly salary of fifteen hundred dollars upon this family of his nephew, "Papa Charles," one of whom was now about to make a raid upon his picked and particular pears.

CHAPTER TWO.

THE CANON'S PEARS,

When the little girls had left him, Napoleon remained for some moments standing in the mouth of his grotto. His hands were clasped behind his back, his head was bent, his eyes were fixed upon the sea.

This, as I have told you, was a favorite attitude of the little boy, copied from his uncle the canon; it remained his favorite attitude through life, as almost any picture of this remarkable man will convince you.

The boy was always thoughtful. But this day he was especially so. For he knew that it was his birthday; and while not so much notice was taken of children's birthdays when Napoleon was a boy as is now the custom, still a birthday *was* a birthday.

So the day set the little fellow to thinking; and, young as he was, he had yet much to remember.

He felt that he ought to be as rich and important as the other boys whom he knew round about Ajaccio There were Andrew Pozzo and Charles Abbatucci, for example. They had everything they wished, their fathers were rich and powerful; and they made fun of him, calling him "little frowsy head," and "down at the heel," just because his mother could not always look after his clothes, and keep him neat and clean.

Napoleon could not see why they should be better off than was he. His father, Charles Bonaparte, was, he had heard them say at home, a count, but of what good was it to be a count, or a duke, if one had not palaces and treasure to show for it?

Napoleon knew that the big and bare four-story house in which he lived was by no means a palace; and so far from having any treasures to spend, he knew, instead, that if it were not for the help of their uncle, the Canon Lucien, they would often go hungry in the big house on the little park.

But there was one consolation. If he was badly off, so, too, were many other boys and girls in that Mediterranean island. For when Napoleon Bonaparte was a boy, there was much trouble in Corsica. That rocky, sea-washed, forest-crowned island of mountains and valleys, queer customs and brave people, had been in rebellion, against its masters - first, the republic of Genoa, and then against France.

Napoleon's father, Charles Bonaparte, had been a Corsican politician and patriot, a follower of the great Corsican leader, Paoli, who had spent many years of a glorious life in trying to lead his fellow-Corsicans to liberty and self-government. But the attempt had been a failure; and three months before the baby Napoleon was born, Charles Bonaparte had, with other Corsican leaders, given up the struggle. He submitted to the French power, took the oath of allegiance, and became a French citizen. And thus it came to pass that little Napoleon Bonaparte, though an Italian by blood and family, was really by birth a French citizen.

Still, all that did not help him much, if, indeed, he thought anything about it as he stood in his grotto looking out to sea. He was thinking of other things, - of how he would like to be great and strong and rich, so that he could be a leader of other boys, rather than be teased by them; for little Napoleon Bonaparte did not take kindly to being teased, but would get very angry at his tormentors, and would bite and scratch and fight like any little savage. He had, as a child, what is known as an ungovernable temper, although he was able to keep it under control until the moment came when he could both say and do to his own satisfaction. He loved his father and mother; he loved his brothers and sisters; he loved his uncle, the Canon Lucien; he loved, more than all his other playmates and companions, his boy-uncle, fat, twelve-year-old Joey Fesch, who had taught him his letters, and been his admirer and follower from babyhood.

But though he loved them all, he loved his own way best; and he was bound to have it, however much his father might talk, his mother chide, or his uncle the canon correct him. So, as he stood in the grotto, remembering that on that day he was seven years old, he determined to let all his family see that he knew what he wished to become and do. He would show them, he declared, that he was a little boy, a baby, no longer; they should know that he was a boy who would be a man long before other boys grew up, and would then show his family that they had never really understood him.

At last he turned away and walked slowly toward home. The Bonaparte house was, as I have told you, a big, bare, four-story, yellow-gray house. It stood on a little narrow street, now called, after Napoleon's mother, Letitia Place, in the town of Ajaccio. The street was not over eight or ten feet wide; but opposite to the house was a little park that allowed the Bonapartes to get both light and air - something that would otherwise be hard to obtain in a street only ten feet wide.

Tired and thirsty from his walk through the sunshine of the hot August afternoon, the boy started for the dining-room for a drink of water. As he opened the door in his quick, impetuous way, he heard a noise as of some one startled and fleeing. The swinging sash of the long French window opposite him shut with a bang, and Napoleon had a glimpse of a bit of white skirt, caught for an instant on the window-fastening.

"Ah, ha! it was not a bird, then, that fluttering," he said. "It was a girl. One of my sisters. Now, which one, I wonder? and why did she run? I do not care to catch her. It is no sport playing with girls."

So little curiosity did he have in the matter, that he did not follow on the track of the fugitive, nor even go to the window to look out; but, walking up to the sideboard, he opened it to take the water-pitcher and get a drink.

As he did so, he started. There stood the basket of fruit which Saveria had filled so carefully with fruit for his uncle the canon. But now the basket was only half filled. Who had taken the fruit?

He clapped his hands together in surprise; for the fruit of his uncle the canon was something no one in the house dared to touch. Punishment swift and sure would descend upon the culprit.

"But, look!" he said half-aloud; "who has dared to touch the fruit of my uncle the canon? Touch it? My faith! they have taken half of it. Ah, that skirt! Could it have been - it must have been one of my sisters. But which one?"

As he stood thus wondering, his eyes still fixed upon the rifled basket of fruit, he heard behind him a voice that tried to be harsh and stern, calling his name.

"Napoleon!" cried the new-comer, "what are you doing at the sideboard? and why have you opened it? You know we have forbidden you to take anything to eat before mealtime. What have you done?"

It was the voice of his uncle, the Canon Lucien. Napoleon, turning at the question, met the glance of his uncle fastened upon him. The Canon Lucien Bonaparte was a funny looking, fat little man, as bald as he was good-natured, - and that was *very* bald, - and with a smooth, ordinary-appearing face, only remarkable for the same sharp, eagle-like look that marked his nephew Napoleon when he, too, became a man.

Napoleon looked at his uncle the canon with indignation and denial on his face. "Why, my uncle, I have taken nothing!" he declared.

Then suddenly he remembered how he had been discovered by his uncle standing before the half-emptied basket of fruit. Could it be that the old gentleman suspected him of pilfering? Would he dare accuse him of the crime?

At the thought his face flushed red and hot. For you must know, boys and girls, that sometimes the fear of being suspected of a misdeed, even when one is absolutely innocent, brings to the face the flush that is considered a sign of guilt, and thus people are misunderstood and wrongfully accused. When one is high-spirited this is more liable to occur. It was so, at this moment, with the little Napoleon. His confused air, his flushed face, even his look of indignant denial, joined as evidence against him so strongly that his uncle the canon said sharply, "Come, you, Napoleon! do not lie to me now."

At that remark all the boy's pride was on fire.

"I never lie, uncle; you know I never lie!" he cried hotly.

But Uncle Lucien was so certain of the boy's guilt that he mistook his pride for impudence. And yet he was such a good-natured old fellow, and loved his nieces and nephews so dearly, that he tried to soften and belittle the theft of his precious fruit.

"No harm is done," he said, "if you but tell me what you have done. The fruit can be replaced, and I will say nothing, though you know you are forbidden to meddle with my fruit. But I do not love to see you doing wrong. I will not tolerate a lie. I do not know just what you have done; but if you will tell me the truth, I will - of course I will - pardon you. Why did you take my fruit?"

"I took nothing, uncle," the boy declared. "It was" - then he stopped. Suppose it had been taken by one of his sisters, or by Panoria, their guest? The flutter of the departing skirt, as he came into the room, assured him it was one of these. But which one? And why should he accuse the little girls? It was not manly, and he wished to be a man.

More than this, he was angry to think that he had been suspected, more angry yet to think he had been accused by good Uncle Lucien, and furiously angry to think that his word was doubted; so he said nothing further.

"Ah, so! It was - you, then," the canon said, shaking his head in sorrowful belief.

"No; I did not say so!" exclaimed Napoleon. "It was not I."

"Take care, take care, my son," the canon said, very nearly losing his temper over what he considered Napoleon's insincerity. "You cannot deceive me. See! look at yourself in the glass. Your face betrays you. It is red with shame."

"Then is my color a liar, uncle; but I am not," Napoleon insisted.

"What were you doing here, all alone?" asked his uncle.

"I was thirsty," replied the nephew. "I did but come for a drink of water."

"That perhaps is so," said Uncle Lucien. "There is no harm in that. You came for a drink of water; but, how was it after that, - eh, my friend?"

"That is all, uncle," replied Napoleon.

"And the water? Have you taken a drink of it, yet?"

"No, uncle; not yet."

The canon again shook his head doubtingly.

"See, then," he declared, "you came for a drink of water. You took no drink; the sideboard stands open; my fruit has disappeared. Napoleon, this is not right. You have done a wrong. Come, tell me the truth. If it is not as you say, if you have lied to me, much as I love you, I will have you punished. It is wicked in you, and I will not be merciful."

As the canon said this with raised voice and warning finger, Napoleon's father, "Papa Charles," entered the room. With him came Napoleon's brother Joseph, two years older than he, and his twelve-year-old uncle-Joey Fesch. Joey was Mamma Letitia's half-brother, a Swiss-Corsican boy. He was, as I have told you, Napoleon's firm supporter.

They looked in surprise at Uncle Lucien and Napoleon, and would have inquired as to the meaning of the attitude of the two. But the fact was, Napoleon had so many such moments of rebellion, that they gave it no immediate thought; and just then Charles Bonaparte had a serious political question which he wished to refer to the Canon Lucien.

The two men at once began talking; the two boys saw through the open window something that engaged their attention, and Napoleon was unnoticed. But still the little boy stood, too proud to move away, too angry to speak, and so filled with a sense of the injustice that was done him, that he remained with downcast eyes, almost rooted to the spot, while still the sideboard stood open, and the tell-tale basket stood despoiled within it. The door opened again, and Saveria entered hastily. She went to the sideboard, took out the basket of fruit, and then you may be sure there was an exclamation that attracted the attention of all in the room.

"For mercy's sake!" she cried. "Who has taken the canon's fruit?"

"Ah, yes, who?" echoed Uncle Lucien, wheeling about, and laying his hand upon Napoleon's shoulder. "Behold, Saveria! here is the culprit. He has taken my fruit."

Napoleon pushed away his uncle's hand.

"It is not so!" he said; but he grew pale as he spoke. "I have not touched it."

"But some one has. Hear me, Saveria!" the canon commanded; for in that house he had quite as much to say as the Father and Mother Bonaparte. "Call in the other children. We will soon settle this."

All were soon in the room, - the two little girls, Joseph, and Uncle Joey Fesch, even baby Lucien, who was named for his uncle the canon. The children made a charming group; but they looked at Napoleon with curiosity and surprise, wondering into what new trouble he had fallen. For the solemn manner in which they had been called together, the grave looks of Papa Charles, of Uncle Lucien, and of Nurse Saveria, led them all to believe that something really serious had happened in the Bonaparte household.

CHAPTER THREE.

THE ACCUSATION.

"Now, then, children, listen to me, and answer, he who is the guilty one," Charles Bonaparte said, facing the group of children. "Who is it that has taken the fruit from the basket of your uncle the canon?"

Each child declared his or her innocence, though one might imagine that Eliza's voice was not so outspoken as the others.

"And what do you say, Napoleon?" asked Papa Charles, turning toward the suspected one.

"I have already said, Papa Charles, that it was not I," Napoleon answered, this time calmly and coolly; for his composure had returned.

"That is a lie, Napoleon!" exclaimed Nurse Saveria, who, as the trusted servant of the Bonaparte family, spoke just as she wished, and said precisely what she meant, while no one questioned her freedom. "That is a lie, Napoleon, and you know it!" The boy sprang toward the nurse in a rage, and, lifting his hand threateningly, cried, "Saveria! if you were not a woman, I would" - and he simply shook his little fist at her, too angry even to complete his threat.

"How now, Napoleon! what would you do?" his father exclaimed.

But Saveria only laughed scornfully. "It must have been you, Napoleon," she said. "I have not left the pantry since I placed the basket of fruit in this sideboard. No one has come in through the door except you and your uncle the canon. Who else, then, could have taken the fruit? You will not say" - and here she laughed again - "that it is your uncle the canon who has stolen his own fruit?"

"Ah, but I wish it had been I," said Uncle Lucien, smiling sadly; for it sorely disturbed his good-nature to have such a scene, and to be a witness of what he believed to be Napoleon's obstinacy and untruthfulness. "I would surely say so, even if I had to go without my supper for the disobedient act."

"But," suggested Napoleon, in a broken voice, touched with the shame of appearing to be a tell-tale, "it is possible for some one to come in here through the window."

"Bah!" cried Saveria. "Do not be a silly too. No one has come through the window. You are the thief, Napoleon. You have taken the fruit. Come, I will punish you doubly - first for thieving, and then for lying."

But as she crossed as if to seize the boy, Napoleon sprang toward his uncle for refuge.

"Uncle Lucien! I did not do it!" he cried. "They must not punish me!"

"Tell the truth, Napoleon," his father said. "That is better than lying."

"Yes, tell the truth, Napoleon," repeated his uncle; "only by confession can you escape punishment."

"Ah, yes; punishment - how does that sound, Napoleon?" whispered Joseph in his ear. "You had better tell the truth. Saveria's whip hurts."

"And so does my hand, rascal!" cried Napoleon, enraged at the taunts of his brother. And he sprang upon Joseph, and beat and bit him so sharply that the elder boy howled for help, and Uncle Joey Fesch was obliged to pull the brothers apart. For Joseph and Napoleon were forever quarrelling; and Uncle Joey Fesch was kept busy separating them, or smoothing over their squabbles.

As Uncle Joey Fesch drew Napoleon away, he said, "Tell them you took the fruit, and they will pardon you. Is it not so, Uncle Lucien?" he added, turning to the canon.

"Assuredly, Joey Fesch," the Canon Lucien replied. "Sin confessed is half forgiven."

But Napoleon only stamped his foot. "Why should I confess?" he cried. "What should I confess? I should lie if I did so. I will not lie! I tell you I did not take any of my uncle's fruit!"

"Confess," urged Joseph.

"'Fess," lisped baby Lucien.

"Confess, dear Napoleon," sister Pauline begged.

Only Eliza remained quiet.

"Napoleon," said the Canon Lucien, who, as head of the Bonaparte family, and who, especially because he was its main support, was given leadership in all home affairs, "we waste time with you; for you are but an obstinate boy. At first I felt sorry for you, and would have excused you, but now I can do so no longer. See, now; I give you five minutes by my watch in which to confess your wrong-doing. You ask for my protection. I am certain of your guilt. But I open a door of escape. It is the door to pardon; it is confession. Profit by it. See, again," - here the canon took out his watch, - "it is now five minutes before seven. If, when the clock strikes seven, you have not confessed, Saveria shall give you a whipping. Am I right, brother Charles?"

"You are right, Canon," replied Papa Charles. "If within five minutes by your watch Napoleon has not confessed, Saveria shall give him the whip."

"The whip is for horses and dogs, but not for boys," Napoleon declared, upon whom this threat of the whip always had an extraordinary effect. "I am not a beast."

"The whip is for liars, Napoleon," returned Papa Charles; "for liars and children who disobey."

"Then, you are cruel to lay it over me; you are cruel and unjust," declared the boy. "For I am not a liar; I am not disobedient. I will not be whipped!"

As he spoke, the boy's eyes flashed defiance. He crossed his arms on his breast, lifted his head proudly, planted himself sturdily on his feet, and flung at them all a look of mingled indignation and determination.

Supper was ready; and the family, all save Napoleon, seated themselves at the table. The five minutes granted him by the canon had run into a longer time, when little Pauline, distressed at sight of her brother standing pale and grave in front of the open sideboard and the despoiled basket of fruit, rose from her chair; approaching him, she whispered, "Poor boy! they will give you the whip. I am sure of it. Hear me! While they are not looking, run away. See! the window is open."

"Run away? Not I!" came Napoleon's answer in an indignant whisper. "I am not afraid."

"But I am," said Pauline. "I do not wish them to whip you. I shall cry. Run, Napoleon! run away!"

The perspiration stood in beads on the boy's sallow forehead; but he said nothing. "Ask Uncle Lucien's pardon, Napoleon; ask Papa Charles's pardon, if you will not run away," Pauline next whispered; "or let me. Come! may I not do it for you?"

Napoleon's hand dropped upon Pauline's shoulder, as if to keep her back from such an action; but he said nothing.

"Pauline, leave your brother," Charles Bonaparte said. "He is a stubborn and undutiful boy. I forbid you to speak to him."

Then turning to his son, he said, "Napoleon, we have given you more than the time offered you for reflection. Now, sir, come and ask pardon for your misdeed, and all will be over."

"Yes, come," said Uncle Lucien.

Napoleon remained silent.

"Do you not hear me, Napoleon?" his father said.

"Yes, papa," replied the boy.

"Well?"

Pauline pushed her brother; but he would not move. "Go! do go!" she said. Instead, Napoleon drew away from her. Uncle Joey Fesch took Napoleon by the arm, and sought to draw him toward the table. Even Joseph rose and beckoned him to come. But the boy made no motion toward the proffered pardon.

"Stupid boy! Obstinate pig!" cried Joseph; "why do you not ask pardon?"

"Because I have done no evil," replied Napoleon. "You are the stupid one; you are the pig, I say. Did I not tell you I did not touch the fruit?"

"Still obstinate!" exclaimed "Papa Charles," turning away from his son. "He does not wish for pardon. He is wicked. Saveria! take this headstrong boy to the kitchen, and lay the whip upon him well, do you hear? He has deserved it."

Napoleon fled to the corner, and stood at bay. Uncle Joey Fesch joined him, as if to protect and defend him. But when big and strong Nurse Saveria bore down upon them both, Uncle Joey, after an unsuccessful attempt to drag Napoleon with him, turned from the enemy, and sprang through the open window.

Then Saveria flung her arms about the little Napoleon, and, in spite of his kickings and scratchings, bore him from the room, while all laughed except Pauline. She stuffed her fingers into her ears to shut out the sound of her brother's cries. But she had no need to do this. No sound came from the punishment chamber. For not a sound, not a cry, not even a sigh, escaped from the boy who was bearing an unmerited punishment.

CHAPTER FOUR.

BREAD AND WATER.

You will, no doubt, wonder what Napoleon's mother was doing while her little son was undergoing his unjust punishment. Perhaps if she had been at home things would not have turned out so badly with the boy; for "Mamma Letitia," as the Bonaparte children called their beautiful mother, had a way about her that none of them could resist. She had much more will and spirit, she saw things clearer and better, than did "Papa Charles."

Indeed, Napoleon said when he was a man, recalling the days of his boyhood in Ajaccio, "I had to be quick when I wished to do anything naughty, for my Mamma Letitia would always restrain my warlike temper; she would not put up with my defiance and petulance. Her tenderness was severe, meting out punishment and reward with equal justice, - merit and demerit, she took both into account."

So, you see, she would probably have understood that Napoleon spoke the truth, and that it was some one else who had taken the fruit from the basket of their uncle the canon. But Mamma Letitia was not at home. She had gone to Melilli, in the country beyond Ajaccio, to visit her mother and step-father - the father and mother of her half-brother, "Uncle Joey Fesch," as the Bonaparte children called him. Melilli was in the midst of fields and forests and luscious vineyards, and it was a great treat for the children to go there to visit their grandmother.

Sometimes their mother would take one or two of the children with her; but on this visit she had gone alone. That very evening her husband was to join her, and there had been great contention among the children as to which of them should accompany their father.

Before leaving the supper-table "Papa Charles" announced that their Uncle Santa's carriage would be at the door in half an hour; that Uncle Joey Fesch would drive; and that Joseph and Lucien and Eliza - "the good children," as he called them - should go with him to Melilli to visit their Grandmother Fesch, and bring back Mamma Letitia. Joseph exulted loudly; Eliza said nothing; and baby Lucien crowed his delight. But Pauline slipped out into the pantry where Napoleon stood silent and still defiant. "I am to stay with you, brother," she said. "Will you be good to me?"

Napoleon slipped his arm about his little sister's neck; but just then his father came from the dining-room, and the boy drew up again, haughty and hard.

"Well, Napoleon," said his father, stopping an instant before the boy, "I hope you are sorry and subdued. Will you now ask your Uncle Lucien's pardon?"

Napoleon looked his father full in the face. "I did not take that fruit, papa," he said.

"What! stubborn still?" his father cried. "See, then; it

shall not be said in my home that an obstinate little fellow like you can rule the house. Since the whip has not conquered you, we will try what starving will do. Listen! I am to go to Melilli for Mamma Letitia. Joseph, Eliza, and Lucien, our three good ones, shall go with me; we shall be gone for three days. As for you, Napoleon, you shall remain here, and shall have only bread and water, unless, indeed, before our return you ask pardon from your uncle the canon."

Pauline looked sadly at Napoleon, and caught his hand. Then she asked her father, "But he may have a little cheese with his bread, may he not, papa?"

"Well - yes" - her father yielded. "But only common cheese, Pauline; not broccio."

Now, broccio was the favorite cheese of the Corsican children, and Pauline protested.

"Oh, yes, papa! let him have broccio, papa," she said. "Why, broccio is the best cheese in Corsica!"

"And that is why Napoleon shall not have it," replied her father. "Broccio is for good boys and girls; and Napoleon is not good."

As he said this he glanced at Napoleon sharply, as if he really hoped for and expected a word of repentance, a look of entreaty. But Napoleon said nothing. He looked even more haughty and unyielding than ever; and his father, with a word of farewell only to Pauline, left the room.

"Poor Napoleon," said Pauline pityingly, as their father closed the door. "See, I will stay by you. But why will you not ask for pardon?"

"Because pardon is for the guilty, Pauline," Napoleon replied; "and I am not guilty."

"And will you never ask it?"

"Never," her brother said firmly.

"But, O Napoleon!" cried the little girl, "what if they should always give you just bread and water and cheese?"

"And if they should, I would not give in," Napoleon answered. "What can I do? I am not master here."

Pauline gave a great sigh of sympathy. The thought of never having anything to eat but bread and water and a little cheese was too much for her courage.

"I could confess anything, rather," she said. "I would ask pardon three times a day."

"And I would not," said Napoleon. "But then, I am a man."

Just then the three children who were to accompany their father to Milelli, passed through the pantry, for they had been to bid Nurse Saveria good-by. Joseph caught the last word.

"A man, are you!" he cried. "Then, why not be a man, and not a baby?"

"Bah, rascal! and who is the greater baby?" his brother responded. "It is he who cries the loudest when things go wrong; and I never cry."

Joseph said nothing further except, "Good-by, obstinate one!"

"Good-by," lisped baby Lucien.

But Eliza said nothing. She did not even glance at Napoleon as she passed him; and he simply looked at her, without a word of accusation or farewell.

The three days passed quietly, though hungrily, for Napoleon. Uncle Lucien said nothing to influence the boy, though he looked sadly, and sometimes wistfully, at him; and Pauline tried to sweeten the bread and water and cheese as much as possible by her sympathy and companionship.

Of this last, however, Napoleon did not wish much. He spent much of the time in his grotto, brooding over his wrongs, and thinking how he would act if people tried to treat him thus when he became a man.

The second day he dragged his toy cannon to his grotto, and made believe he was a Corsican patriot, intrenched in his fortifications, and holding the whole French army at bay; for though Corsica was a French possession, the people were still smarting under their wrongs, and hated their French oppressors, as they termed them. Some years after, when he was a young man, Napoleon, talking about the home of his boyhood and the troubles of Corsica, said, "I was born while my country was dying. Thirty thousand French thrown upon our shores, drowning the throne of liberty in blood - such was the horrid sight that first met my view. The cries of the dying, the groans of the oppressed, tears of despair, surrounded my cradle at my birth."

It was not quite as bad as all that. But Napoleon liked to use big words and dramatic phrases. It had been, in fact, very much like this before Napoleon was born. He had heard all the stories of French tyranny and Corsican courage, and, like a true Corsican, was hot with wrath against the enslavers of his country, as he called the French. So he found an especial pleasure in bombarding all France with his toy gun from his grotto; and as he then felt very bitter indeed because of his treatment at home, you may be sure the French army was horribly butchered in the boy's make-believe battle before Napoleon's grotto.

Then he went back for his bread and water.

As he approached the house, he found that he was beginning to rebel at the bread and water diet.

Bread and water alone, with just a little cheese, begin to grow monotonous to a healthy boy with a good appetite, after two or three days.

Suddenly Napoleon had a brilliant idea. "The shepherd boys!" he exclaimed.

He hurried to the house, took from Saveria the bread she had put aside for him, and was speedily out of the house again.

This time he took his way to the grazing-lands, where, upon the slopes of the grand mountains that wall in the town of Ajaccio, the shepherd boys were tending their scattered herds.

"Who will exchange chestnut bread for the best town bread in Ajaccio?" he demanded. "I will give piece for piece."

Those shepherd boys led a lonely sort of life, and welcomed anything that was novel. Then, too, they were as tired of their bread, made from pounded chestnuts, as was Napoleon of Saveria's wheat bread.

So Napoleon found a ready response to his offer.

"Here! I'll do it!" - "and I" - "and I" - "and I" - came the answers, in such numbers that Napoleon saw that his little stock would soon be exhausted; and, indeed, he was not overfond of chestnut bread.

So he improved on his idea.

"Piece for piece, I will exchange, as I offered," he announced. "But there are too many of you. See! he who will give me the biggest slice of broccio shall have first choice for the bread, and the next biggest, the next."

This put a different face on the transaction, but it added spice to the operation; and Napoleon actually succeedded in getting for his stale home bread, goodly sized pieces of fresh chestnut bread, and enough of the much-loved broccio, and bunches of luscious grapes, "to boot," to provide him with a generous meal. But the next day the shepherd boys rebelled; they told Napoleon that his bread was stale, and not good. They preferred their chestnut bread.

"But if you will look after our sheep while we go into the town," said one of them, "we will give you some of our bread."

This, however, did not suit Napoleon. "I am not one to tend sheep," he answered. "Keep your bread. It is not so good that one wishes to eat it twice; and - here, I pity you for having always to eat that stuff. Take mine!" With that, he tossed his store of dry bread to the shepherd boys, and, walking back to town, ran in to visit his foster mother; that is, the woman who had been his nurse when he was a baby.

Nurse Camilla, as he called her, or sometimes "foster-mamma Camilla," was now the widow Ilari; but since her husband had been killed in one of those terrible family quarrels known as a Corsican *vendetta*, she had lived in a little house on one of the narrow streets of Ajaccio, not far from the Bonapartes.

She was very fond of her baby, as she called Napoleon; and when he told her of his disgrace at home, she said, -

"Bah! the sillies! Do they not know a truth-teller when they see one? And so they would keep you on bread and water? Not if Nurse Camilla can prevent it. See, now! here is a plenty to eat, and just what my own boy likes, does he not? Eat, eat, my son, and never mind the stale bread of that stingy Saveria."

Then she petted and caressed the boy she so adored; she gave him the best her house afforded, and sent him away to his own home satisfied and filled, but especially jubilant, I fear, because he had got the best, as he termed it, of the home tyranny, and shown how he was able to do for himself even when he was driven to extremities.

It was this ability to use all the conditions of life for his own benefit, and to turn even privation and defeat into victory, that gave to Napoleon, when he became a man, that genius of mastery that made this neglected boy of Corsica the foremost man of all the world.

CHAPTER FIVE.

A WRONG RIGHTED.

It was the third day of the family's absence from the Bonaparte house. Napoleon had been at his favorite resort, - the grotto that overlooked the sea. He had been brooding over his fancied wrongs, as well as his real ones; he had wished he could be a man to do as he pleased. He would free Corsica from French tyranny, make his father rich, and his mother free from worry, and, in fact, accomplish all those impossible things that every boy of spirit and ambition is certain he could do if he might but have the chance.

As he approached his home, he saw little Panoria swinging on the gate. She was waiting for her friend Eliza; for she had learned from Pauline that the absent ones were to return that evening from their visit to Melilli.

Panoria, as you have learned, was a bright little girl, who spoke her mind, and had no great awe for the Bonapartes - not even for the mighty Canon Lucien, the all-powerful Nurse Saveria, nor the masterful little Napoleon.

In fact, Napoleon stood more in awe of Panoria than she did of him. For the boy was, as boys and girls say today, "sweet on" the little Panoria, to whom he gave the pet name "La Giacommetta." Many a battle royal he had fought because of her with the fun-loving boys of Ajaccio, who found that it enraged Napoleon to tease him about the little girl, and therefore never let the opportunity slip to tease and torment him.

"Ah, Napoleon, it is you!" cried Panoria, as the boy approached her. "And what great stories have you been telling yourself today in your grotto?"

"I tell no great stories to myself, little one," Napoleon replied with rather a lordly air. "I do but talk truth with myself."

"Then should you talk truth with me, boy," the little lady replied, a trifle haughty also. "I am not to be called 'little one' by such a mite as you. See! I am taller than you!"

"Yes; when one stands on a gate, one is taller than he who stands on the ground," Napoleon admitted. "But when we stand back to back, who then is the taller? See! Call Pauline! She shall tell us!"

"That shall she not, then," said the little girl, who loved to tease quite as well as most girls. "It would be better to go and make yourself look fine, than to stand here saying how big you are. Go look in the glass. Your stockings are tumbling over your shoes, and your jacket is all awry. How will your Mamma Letitia like that? Run, then! I hear the carriage wheels! In with you, little Down-at-the-heel!"

Smarting under the girl's teasing, and all the more because it came from her, Napoleon sulked into

Eugenie Foa

the house.

But Panoria still swung on the gate. When the carriage stopped before the house, she ran to welcome her friend Eliza, and, with the returned family, entered the house.

In the doorway the fat little canon, Uncle Lucien, received them.

"Back again, uncle!" cried Mamma Letitia in welcome. "And how do you all? Where is Napoleon? Where is Pauline?" The woman who spoke was Madame Letitia Bonaparte, the mother of Napoleon. She was a remarkable woman - remarkable for beauty, for ability, and for position. Born a peasant, she became the mother of kings and queens; reared in poverty, she became the mistress of millions. In her Corsican home she was house-mother and care-taker; and when, made great by her great son, she had every comfort and every luxury, she still remained house-mother and care-taker, looking after her own household, and refusing to spend the money with which her son provided her, for fear that some day she or her family might need it. In all the troubles in Corsica she accompanied her husband to the mountain-retreat and the battle-field, encouraging him by her bravery, and urging him to patriotic purpose, until the end came, and Corsica was defeated and conquered. She carried all the worries and bore all the responsibilities of the Bonaparte household; and it was only by her management and carefulness that the family was kept from absolute poverty.

Her children loved her; but they feared her too, and never thought of going contrary to her desires or commands. Late in life Napoleon once told a boy of whom he was fond the consequences of the only time he ever dared make fun of "Mamma Letitia."

"Pauline and I tried it," he said; "but it was a great mistake on our part. It was the only time in my life that my mother herself ever whipped me. I don't believe Pauline ever forgot it. I never did."

So it was Mamma Letitia who first spoke on the arrival at home; and her first question was as to the children who had remained behind.

"Where is Napoleon? Where is Pauline?" she asked.

Little Pauline sprang from behind her uncle the canon.

"I am here, mamma," she said, and threw herself in her mother's arms.

"But where is Napoleon?"

"He has not been good, mamma," Pauline replied. "See! he is there, behind the door. He dare not come out. He pouts."

"It is not so, mamma," said Napoleon, coming forward; "I do dare. I am sad; but I do not pout."

"And is he obstinate still, Uncle Lucien?" Papa Charles asked. "Has he confessed, or asked your pardon?"

"He has done neither," Uncle Lucien replied. "I have never seen, in any child, such obstinacy as his."

"Napoleon! Obstinacy!" exclaimed Mamma Letitia.

"Why, tell me; what has the boy done?"

Then Uncle Lucien told the story of the rifled basket of fruit, excusing the lad as much as he could, although it must be confessed that the kind of canon was considerably "put out" by the reason of what he called Napoleon's obstinacy.

When, however, he reached the part of his story that described how he wished Napoleon to confess his misdeed, little Panoria, having, as I have told you, none of that awe of the Canon Lucien that his grand nephews and nieces had, burst in upon him, -

"Why, then!" she cried, "I should not think Napoleon would confess. Poor boy! He did not eat your fruit, Canon Lucien."

"How, child! What do you say?" the canon exclaimed. "He did not? Who did, then?"

"Why, I did - and Eliza," Panoria replied

"You - and Eliza!" - "Eliza!" - "Why, she said nothing!" These were the exclamations of surprise and query that came from all present.

"Why, surely!" said Panoria; "and was it wrong? Fruit is free to all here in Corsica. But Eliza was so afraid of her uncle the canon's fruit that I dared her to take some; and we did. Napoleon never touched it. He knew nothing of it."

"My poor boy my good child!" said the Canon Lucien, taking Napoleon in his arms. "Why did you not tell me this?"

"I thought it might have been Eliza who did it," replied the boy; "but I am no tattle-tale, uncle. Besides, I would have said nothing on Panoria's account. She did not lie."

"No more did Eliza," said Joseph.

"Bah, imbecile!" said Napoleon, turning on his brother. "Where, then, is the difference between telling a lie and acting one by keeping quiet, if both mislead?"

You can readily believe that Napoleon was made much of by all his family because of his action. "That is the stuff that makes brave soldiers, leaders, and patriots, my son," his "Mamma Letitia" said. "Would that we all had more of it!"

For Madame Bonaparte knew that there was but little of the heroic in her handsome husband, "Papa Charles." He would flame out with wrath, and tell every one how much he meant to do against tyranny and wrong; he would even act with courage for a while; but at last his love of ease and his dislike of trouble would get the better of his valor, and he would give up the struggle, bow before his opponents, and seek to gain by subserviency their favor and patronage.

As for Eliza, she received a merited punishment - first, for her disobedience in taking what she had been told never to touch; next, for her bravado in daring to act insolently toward her uncle, the canon; then for her gluttony in eating so much of the fruit; and finally, for her "bad heart," as her mother called it, for allowing her brother to suffer in her stead, and be punished for the wrong that she had committed.

As for Napoleon, I fear that this little incident in his life made him feel more important than ever. He assumed a yet more masterful tone toward his companions and playmates, lorded it over Joseph, his brother, and made repeated demands for loyalty upon Uncle Joey Fesch.

But he did feel grateful toward Panoria for her timely word and generous conduct. He became more fond than ever of "La Giacommeta;" and he brought her fruit and flowers, told her of all the great things he meant to do "when he was a man," and even invited her into his much loved and jealously guarded grotto; and that, you may be sure, was a very great favor for Napoleon to grant. For his grotto was his own private and exclusive hermitage.

CHAPTER SIX.

THE BATTLE WITH THE SHEPHERD BOYS.

The relations between Napoleon and the shepherd boys of the Ajaccio hillsides were not improved by his unsatisfactory food-trade during his bread-and-water days.

Whenever he took his walks abroad in their direction, the belligerent shepherd boys made haste to annoy and attack him. They had no special love for the town boys; there was, in fact, a long-standing rivalry and quarrel between them, as there often is between boys of different sections, or between boys of the country and the town.

So you may be sure that Napoleon's solitary tramps along the hillsides were often disturbed and made unpleasant.

At last he determined upon the punishment or discomfiture of the shepherd boys. He roused his playmates to action; and one day they sallied forth in a body, to surprise and attack the shepherd boys. But there must have been a traitor in the camp of the town boys; for, when they reached the hill pastures, they not only found the shepherd boys prepared for them, but they found them arrayed in force. Before the town boys could rush to the attack, the shepherd boys, eager for the fray, "took the initiative," as the war records say, and making a dash upon the town boys, drove them ignominiously from the field.

Napoleon disliked a check. Discomfited and mortified, he turned on big Andrew Pozzo, the leader of the town boys.

"Why, you are no general!" he cried. "You should have massed us all together, and held up firm against the shepherds. But, instead, you scattered us all; and as for you - you ran faster than any of us!"

"Ho! little gamecock! little boaster!" answered Pozzo hotly. "You know it all, do you not? You'd better try it yourself, Captain Down-at-the-heel."

"And I will, then!" cried Napoleon. "Come, boys, try it again! Shall we be whipped by a lot of shepherd boys, garlic lovers, eaters of chestnut bread? Never! Follow me!" But the town boys had received all they wished, for one day. Only a portion of them followed Napoleon's lead; and they turned about and fled before they even met the shepherd boys, so formidable seemed the array of those warriors of the hills.

"Why, this will never do!" Napoleon exclaimed. "It must not be said that we town boys have been whipped into slavery by these miserable ones of the mountains. At them again! What! You will not? Then let us arrange a careful plan of attack, and try them another day. Will you do so?"

The boys promised; for it is always easy to agree to do a thing at some later day. But Napoleon did not intend that the matter should be given up or postponed. He went to his grotto, and carefully thought out a plan of campaign.

The next day he gathered his forces about him, and endeavored to fire their hearts by a little theatrical effect.

"What say you, boys, to a cartel?" he said.

"A cartel?"

"Yes; a challenge to those miserable ones of the hill, daring them to battle."

"But those hill dwellers cannot read; do you not know that, you silly?" Andrew Pozzo cried. "How, then, can you send a challenge?"

"How but by word of mouth?" replied Napoleon. "See, here are Uncle Joey Fesch and big Ilari; they shall go with their sticks, and stand before those shepherd boys, and shall cry aloud" -

"Shall we, then?" broke in big Ilari. "I will do no crying."

Napoleon said nothing. He simply looked at the big fellow - looked at him - and went on as if there had been no interruption, -

"And shall cry aloud, 'Holo, miserable ones! holo, rascal shepherds! The town boys dare you to fight them. Are you cowards, or will you meet them in battle?' This shall Uncle Joey Fesch cry out. He has a mighty voice."

"And of course they will fight," sneered Andrew Pozzo. "Did you think they would not? But shall we?"

"Shall we not, then?" answered Napoleon. "And if you will but follow and obey me, we will conquer those hill boys, as you never could if Pozzo led you on. For I will show you the trick of mastery. Of mastery, do you hear? And those miserable boys of the sheep pastures shall never more play the victor over us boys of the town."

It was worth trying, and the boys of that day and time were accustomed to give and take hard knocks.

So Uncle Joey Fesch and big Tony Ilari, the bearers of the challenge, set off for the hill pastures; and while they were gone Napoleon directed the preparations of his forces.

The heralds returned with an answer of defiance from the hill boys.

"So! they boast, do they?" little Napoleon said. "We will show them how skill is better than strength. Remember my orders: stones in your pockets, the stick in your hand. Attention! In order! March!"

In excellent order the little army set out for the hills. In the pastures where they had met defeat the day before they saw the straggling forces of the shepherd boys awaiting them.

"Halt!" commanded the Captain Napoleon.

"Let the challengers go forward again," he directed. "Summon them to surrender, and pass under the yoke.

Tell them we will be masters in Ajaccio."

The big boy challengers obeyed the little leader's command; and as they departed on their mission Napoleon ordered his soldiers to quietly drop the stones they carried in their pockets, in a line where they stood. Then he planted a stick in the ground as a guide-post.

The challengers came rushing back, followed by the jeers and sticks of the hill boys.

"So! they will not yield? Then will we conquer them," Napoleon cried. "In order! Charge!"

And up the slope, brandishing their sticks, charged the town boys.

The hill boys were ready for them. They were bigger and stronger than the town boys, and they expected to conquer by force.

The two parties met. There was a brief rattle of stick against stick. But the hill boys were the stronger, and Napoleon gave the order to retreat.

Down the hill rushed the town boys. After them, pell-mell, came the hill boys, flushed with victory and careless of consequences. Suddenly, as Napoleon reached his guide-post, he shouted in his shrill little voice, "Halt!" And his army, knowing his intentions, instantly obeyed.

"Stones!" he cried, and they scooped up their supply of ammunition.

"About!" They faced the oncoming foe.

"Fire!" came his final order; and, so fast and furious fell the shower of stones upon the surprised and unprepared hill boys, that their victorious columns halted, wavered, turned, broke, and fled.

"Now! upon them! follow them! drive them!" rang out the little Captain Napoleon's swiftly given orders.

They followed his lead. The hill boys, utterly routed, scattered in dismay. One-half of them were captured and held as prisoners, until Napoleon's two big challengers, now acting as commissioners of conquest, received from the hill boys an unconditional surrender, an acknowledgment of the superiority of the town boys, and the humble promise to molest them no more.

This was Napoleon's first taste of victorious war. But ever after he was an acknowledged leader of the boys of Ajaccio. Andrew Pozzo was unceremoniously deposed from his self-assumed post of commander in all street feuds and forays. The old rivalry was a sore point with him, however; and throughout his life he was the bitter and determined opponent of his famous fellow-Corsican, Napoleon. But you may be sure big Tony Ilari and the other boys paid court to the little Bonaparte's ability; while as for Uncle Joey Fesch, he was prouder than ever of his nine-year-old nephew and commander.

CHAPTER SEVEN.

GOOD-BYE TO CORSICA.

Meantime things were going from bad to worse in the Bonaparte home.

Careless "Papa Charles" made but little money, and saved none; all the economy and planning of thrifty "Mamma Letitia" did not keep things from falling behind, and even the help of Uncle Lucien the canon was not sufficient.

Charles Bonaparte had gained but little by his submitssion to the French. The people in power flattered him, and gave him office and titles, but these brought in no money; and yet, because of his position, he was forced to entertain and be hospitable to the French officers in Corsica.

Now, this all took money; and there was but little money in the Bonaparte house to take. So, at last, after much discussion between the father and mother, - the father urging and the mother objecting, - the Bonapartes decided to sell a field to raise money; and you can scarcely understand how bitter a thing this is to a Corsican. To part with a piece of land is, to him, like cutting off an arm. It hurts.

Napoleon heard all of these discussions, and was sadly aware of the poverty of his home. He worried over it; he wished he could know how to help his mother in her struggles; and he looked forward, more earnestly than ever, to the day when he should be a man, or should at least be able to do something toward helping out in his home.

At last things took a turn. Old King Louis of France was dead; young King Louis - the sixteenth of the name - sat on the throne. There was trouble in the kingdom. There was a struggle between the men who wished to better things and those who wished things to stay as they were. Among these latter were the governors of the French provinces or departments. In order to have things fixed to suit themselves, they selected men to represent them in the nation's assembly at Paris.

The governor of Corsica was one of these men; and by flattery and promises he won over to his side Papa Charles Bonaparte, and had him sent to Paris (or rather to Versailles, where the assembly met, not far from Paris) as a delegate from the nobility of Corsica. This sounded very fine; but the truth is, "Papa Charles" was simply nothing more than "the governor's man," to do as he told him, and to work in his interests.

One result of this, however, was that it made things a little easier for the Bonapartes; and it gave them the opportunity of giving to the two older boys, Joseph and Napoleon, an education in France at the expense of the state.

So when Charles Bonaparte was ready to sail to his duties in France, it was arranged that he should take with him Joseph, Napoleon, and Uncle Joey Fesch. Joseph was now eleven years old; Napoleon was nine, and Uncle Joey was fifteen.

Joseph and Uncle Joey were to be educated as priests; Napoleon was to go to the military school at Brienne. But, at first, both the brothers were sent to a sort of preparatory school at Autun.

Napoleon was delighted. He was to go out into the world. He was to be a man; and yet, when the time came, he hated to leave his home. He was fond of his family; indeed, his life was largely given up to remembering and helping his mother and brothers and sisters. He regretted leaving his dear grotto; he was sorry to say good-by to Panoria - his favorite "La Giacommetta." But his future had been decided upon by his father and mother, and he promised to do great things for them when he was old enough to be a captain in the army - even if it were the army of France. For, you see, he was still so earnest a Corsican patriot, that he wished rather to free Corsica than to defend France.

"Who knows?" he boasted one day to Panoria; "perhaps I will become a colonel, and come back here and be a greater man than Paoli. Perhaps I may free Corsica. What would you think of that, Panoria?"

"I should think it funny for a boy who went to school in France to come away and fight France," said practical Panoria.

But Napoleon would not see it in this way. He dreamed of glory, and believed he would yet be able to strike a blow for the freedom of Corsica. At last the day of departure arrived. There was a lingering leave-taking and a sorrowful one. For the first time, the Bonaparte boys were leaving their mother and their home.

"Be good boys," she said to them; "learn all you can, and try to be a credit to your family. Upon you we look for help in the future. Be thrifty, be saving, do not get sick, and remember that, upon your work now, will depend your success in life."

"Good-bye!" cried Nurse Saveria. "When you come back I will have for you the biggest basket of fruit we can pick in the garden of your uncle the canon."

"That you shall, boy," said Uncle Lucien, slipping his last piece of pocket-money into Napoleon's hand. "And take you this, for luck. You will do your best, I know you will, and you'll come back to us a great man. Don't forget your Uncle Lucien, you boy, when you are famous, will you?"

Napoleon smiled through his tears, and made a laughing promise in reply to his uncle's laughing demand. But, for all the fun of the remark, there was yet a strong groundwork of belief beneath this assertion of the Canon Lucien Bonaparte; the old man was a shrewd observer. His friendship for the little Napoleon was strong. And in spite of all the boy's faults, - his temper, his ambition, his sullenness, his carelessness, and his selfishness, - Uncle Lucien still recognized in this nine-year-old nephew an ability that would carry him forward as he grew older.

"Napoleon has his faults," he said, in talking over family matters with Mamma Letitia and Papa Charles the night before the departure for France; "the boy is not perfect - what child is? But those very faults will grow into action as he becomes acquainted with the world. I expect great things of the boy; and mark my words, Letitia and Charles, it is of no use for you to think on Napoleon's fortune or his future. He will make them for himself, and you will look to him for assistance, rather than he to you. Joseph is the eldest son; but, of this I am sure, Napoleon will be the head of this family. Remember what I say; for, though I may not live to see it, some of you will - and will profit by it."

They were all on the dock as the vessel sailed away, bearing Papa Charles, Uncle Joey Fesch, and the two Bonaparte boys, from Ajaccio to Florence.

Mamma Letitia was there, tearful, but smiling, with Eliza, and Pauline, and Baby Lucien; so were Uncle Lucien the canon, and Aunt Manuccia, who had been their mother's housekeeper, with Nurse Saveria, and Nurse Ilaria, whom Napoleon called foster-mother, and even little Panoria, to whom Napoleon cried "Good-by, Giacommeta mia! I'll come back some day."

Then the vessel moved out into the harbor, and sailed away for Italy, while the tearful group on the dock and the tearful group on the deck threw kisses to one another until they could no longer make out faces or forms.

The home tie was broken; and Napoleon Bonaparte, a boy of nine and a half years, was launched upon life - a life the world was never to forget.

CHAPTER EIGHT.

AT THE PREPARATORY SCHOOL.

The Bonaparte boys and their father stopped a while in Florence, so that Charles Bonaparte could procure the proper papers to prove that he was of what is called noble birth. For it seems that only the children of nobles could enter the French military school at Brienne.

He procured these at last, and also a letter of introduction to the French queen, Marie Antoinette whose sad story you all know so well.

Then they set out for Autun, and reached that quaint old town on the last day of the year 1778. On New Year's Day, 1779, Napoleon was entered as a pupil in the preparatory school at Autun.

Autun has been a school town tor hundreds of years. The old Druids had a school there, and so did the Romans. It is one of the oldest of French towns; and you will find it on your map of France, about one hundred and fifty miles south-east of Paris. It is a picturesque old town, placed on a sloping hillside, that runs down to the Arroux River. There is a cathedral in the town over nine hundred years old; and there, too, Napoleon found a college and a seminary, a museum and a library, with plenty of ruins, walls, and gateways, and such things, that told of its great age and old-time grandeur.

It was a fine place in which to go to school, and the Bonaparte boys must have found it quite a change from their Corsican home. The bishop of Autun, who had charge of the cathedral and the schools, was the nephew of a friend of Charles Bonaparte, and he promised to look after the boys.

Napoleon did not stay long in the school at Autun. His father went to Paris to enter upon his duties as delegate to the Assembly, intending, while there, to make arrangements for getting Napoleon into the military school at Brienne.

But there was much need of the preparatory work at Autun. For you must know that, being a Corsican, Napoleon knew scarcely a word of French. The Corsicans speak Italian, and this would never do for a French schoolboy. So, for three months, Napoleon was drilled in French.

He did not take kindly to it. But he did his best. For, you see, his journey from Florence to Marseilles, and on to Autun, had opened his eyes. He saw, for the first time, cities larger than Ajaccio, and learned that there were other places in the world besides Corsica.

But he never really lost his Ajaccio tongue, and for most of his life he talked French with an Italian accent.

It was a queer-looking little Italian boy who was thus studying French at Autun school. You would scarcely have looked at him twice; for his figure was small, his appearance insignificant, his face sober and solemn, his hair stiff and stringy, and his complexion sallow. The boys made fun of the way in which he talked, as boys are apt to make sport of those who do not talk as they do.

"What is your name, new boy?" the big boy of Autun school called out to Napoleon, as on that first day of the new year, which was, as I have said, his first day at school, the Bonaparte brothers wandered about the schoolyard, strangers and shy.

"Na-polle-o-nay!" answered the little new-comer, giving the Corsican pronunciation to his name of Napoleon.

"Oho! so!" cried the big boy, mimicking him. "Na-pailli-au-nez, is it? See, fellows, see! this is Mr. Straw-Nose!"

For, you see, the way Napoleon pronounced his name sounded very much like the French words that mean "the nose of straw." That, of course, gave the boys at the school a rare chance to nickname; and so poor Napoleon was called "Mr. Straw-Nose" all the time he was at that school.

This was not very long, however; for in three months he had made sufficient progress in his study of French to permit him to pass into the military school at Brienne, into which his father was at last able to procure his admission.

But, while he was at Autun, Napoleon seems to have been a favorite with his teachers. One of them, the Abbe Chardon, spoke of him as "a sober, thoughtful child." He wished very much to get into the military school; so he worked hard, learned quickly, and was proud of what he called his ability.

But when the boys tried to plague him, or to twit him for being a Corsican, the boy was ready enough to talk back.

The French boys knew but little about Corsica, and had a certain contempt for the little island which, so they declared, was the home of robbers, and which France had one day gone across and conquered.

"Bah, Corsican!" one of the big boys called out to the new scholar, "and what is Corsica? Just an island of cowards. Just see how we Frenchmen whipped you out of your boots!"

Napoleon clinched his little fist, and turned hotly on his tormentor. But he was already learning the lesson of self-control.

"And how did you do it, Frenchman?" he replied. "By numbers. If you had been but four to one against us, you would never have conquered us. But, behold! you were ten to one! That is too much to struggle against."

"And yet you boast of your general - your leader," said the other boy. "You say he is a fine commander - this - how do you call him? - this Paoli."

"I say so; yes, sir," Napoleon replied sadly. Then, as if his ambition led him on, he added, "I would like to be like him. What could I not do then!"

This feeling of being a Corsican, an outsider at the

school, made the boy quiet and retiring. He kept by himself, just as he had at home when things did not suit him; he walked out alone, and played with no one. To be sure, he was more or less with his brother Joseph, who loved his ease and comfort, did not fire up when the other boys teased him, and smoothed over many a quarrel between them and his brother.

Napoleon would often find fault with Joseph's lack of spirit, as he called it; but Joseph, all through life, liked to take things easy, and hated to face trouble. Most of us do, you know; but it was the readiness of Napoleon to boldly face danger, and to attempt what appeared to be the impossible, that made him the self-reliant boy, the successful man, the conqueror, the emperor, the hero.

CHAPTER NINE

THE LONELY SCHOOL-BOY

While Napoleon was at Autun school, studying French, and preparing for entrance into the military academy, his father, Charles Bonaparte, was at Versailles, trying to get a little more money from the king, in return for his services as Corsica's delegate to France.

At the same time he was working to complete the arrangements which should permit him to enter Napoleon at the military school, at the expense of the state. This he finally accomplished; and on the twenty-third of April, in the year 1779, Napoleon entered the royal military school at Brienne.

There were ten of these military schools in France. They were started as training-schools for boys who were to become officers in the French army. The one at Brienne was a bare and ugly-looking lot of buildings in the midst of trees and gardens, looking down toward the little River Aube, and near to the fine old chateau, or nobleman's house, built, a hundred years before Napoleon's day, by the last Count of Brienne.

There were a hundred and fifty boys at Brienne school, although there was scarcely room enough for a hundred and twenty.

The new-comer was therefore crowded in with the others; and you may be sure that the old boys did not make life pleasant and easy for the new boy.

Although he had learned to write and speak French during his three months' schooling at Autun, he could not, of course, speak it very well; so the boys plagued him for that. And when he told them his name, they, too, made fun of his pronunciation of Na-po-le-one, and at once nicknamed him, "straw-nose," just as the Autun boys had done.

Most of the boys who attended Brienne school were the sons of French noblemen. They had plenty of money to spend; they made a show of it, and dressed and did things as finely as they could. Napoleon, you know, was poor. His father had scrimped and begged and borrowed to send his boys to school. He could not, therefore, give them much for themselves; so the French boys, with the money to spend and the manners to show, made no end of fun of the little Corsican, who had neither money nor manners.

At once he got into trouble. He did not like, nor did he understand, the ways of the French boys; he was alone; he was homesick; and naturally he became sulky and uncompanionable. When the boys teased him, he tossed back a wrathful answer; when they made fun of his appearance, he grew angry and sullen; and when they tried to force him into their society, he went off by himself, and acted like a little hermit.

But when they twitted him on his nationality, called him "Straw-nose, the Corsican," and made all manner of fun of that rocky and (as they called it) savage island, then all the patriotism in the boy's nature was aroused, and he called his tormentors French cowards, with whom he would one day get square.

"Bah, Corsican! and what will you do?" asked Peter Bouquet. "I hope some day to give Corsica her liberty," said Napoleon; "and then all Frenchmen shall march into the sea."

Upon which all the boys laughed loudly; and Napoleon, walking off in disgust, went into the school-building, and there vented his wrath upon a portrait of Choiseul, that hung upon the wall.

"Ah, ha! blackguard, pawnbroker, traitor!" he cried, shaking his fist at this portrait of a stout and smiling-looking gentleman. "I loathe you! I despise you! I spit upon you!" And he did.

Now, Monsieur the Count de Choiseul was the French nobleman who was one of the old King Louis's ministers and advisers. It was he who had planned the conquest of Corsica, and annexed it to France. You may not wonder, then, that the little Corsican, home-sick for his native island, and hot with rage toward those who made fun of it, when he came upon this portrait of the man to whom, as he had been taught, all Corsica's troubles were due, should have vented his wrath upon it, and heaped insults upon it.

Unfortunately for him, however, the teachers at Brienne did not appreciate his patriotic wrath; so, when one of the tattle-tales reported Napoleon's actions, at once he was pounced upon, and ordered to ask pardon for what he had said and done, standing before the portrait of Corsica's enslaver.

He approached the portrait so reluctantly and contemptuously, that one of the teachers scolded him sharply.

"You are not worthy to be a French officer, foolish boy," the teacher declared; "you are no true son of France, thus to insult so great and noble a Frenchman as Monsieur the Count de Choiseul."

"I am a son of Corsica," Napoleon replied proudly; "that noble country which this man ground in the dust."

"As well he might," replied the teacher tauntingly. "He was Corsica's best friend. He was worth a thousand Paoli's."

"It is not so!" cried Napoleon, hot with patriotic indignation. "You talk like all Frenchmen. Paoli was a great man. He loved his country. I admire him. I wish to be like him. I can never forgive my father for having been willing to desert the cause of Corsica, and agree to its union with France. He should have followed Paoli's lead, even though it took him with Paoli, into exile in England."

"Bah! your father!" one of the big boys standing by exclaimed; "and who is your father, Straw-nose?"

Napoleon turned upon his tormentor; "a better man than you, Frenchman!" he cried; "a better man than this Choiseul here. My father is a Corsican."

"A stubborn rebel, this boy," said the teacher, now losing his temper. "What! you will not ask Monsieur the Count's pardon, as a rebel should? Then will we tame your spirit. Is a little arrogant Corsican to defy all

France, and Brienne school besides? Go, sir! We will devise some fine punishment for you, that shall well repay your insolence and disobedience."

So Napoleon, in disgrace, left the schoolroom, and pacing down his favorite walk, the pleasant avenue of chestnut-trees that lined the path from one of the schoolhouse doors, he sought his one retreat and hermitage, - his loved and bravely defended garden.

That garden was a regular Napoleonic idea. I must tell you about it.

CHAPTER TEN.

IN NAPOLEON'S GARDEN.

One of the rules of Brienne school was that each pupil should know something about agriculture. To illustrate this study, each one of the one hundred and fifty boys had a little garden-spot set aside for him to cultivate and keep in order.

Some of the boys did this from choice, and because they loved to watch things grow; but many of them were careless, and had no love for fruit or flowers; so while some of the garden-plots were well kept, others were neglected.

Napoleon was glad of this garden-plot, for it gave him something which he could call his own. He cared for it faithfully; but he wished to make it even more secluded. He remembered his dear grotto at Ajaccio, and studied over a plan to make his garden-plot just such a real retreat. But it was not large enough for this. He looked about him. The boys to whom belonged the garden-plots on either side of him were careless and neglectful. Their gardens received no attention; they were overgrown with weeds; their hedges were full of gaps and holes.

"I will take them," said Napoleon; "what one cannot

care for, another must."

So the boy went systematically to work to "annex" his neighbors' kingdoms, and make from the three plots one ample retreat for himself. He cut down the separating borders; he trimmed and trained and filled in the stout outside hedge, until it completely surrounded his enlarged domain; and, in the centre of the paths and flower-beds and hedges, he put up a seat and a little summer-bower for his pleasure and protection.

It took some time to get this into shape, of course. When he had completed it, and was beginning to enjoy it, the owners of the plots he had confiscated awoke to a sense of their loss and the excellent garden-spot this young Corsican had made for them. "For of course," they said, "the garden-plots are ours. Straw Nose has improved them at his own risk. What he has made we will keep for our own pleasure." So they attempted to occupy their property; but with Napoleon there was force in the old saying, "Possession is nine points of the law."

When the dispossessed boys demanded their property, he refused it; when they spoke of their rights, he laughed at them; and when they attempted to enter the garden by force, he fell upon them, drove them flying from the field, and pommelled them so soundly that they judged discretion to be the better part of valor, and made no further attempt to disturb the conqueror.

The other boys did attempt it, however, simply to tease and annoy the fiery Corsican. But it always resulted in their own damage; for Napoleon become so attached to his garden citadel, that he would grow furiously angry whenever he was disturbed. Rushing out, he would rout his assailants completely; until at last it was understood that it was safest to let him alone.

As he sought his garden on this day of disgrace to which I have referred, he was full of bitter thoughts against the unfriendly boys and the unsympathetic teachers amid whom his lot was cast. Like most boys, he determined to do something that should free him from this tyranny; then, like many boys, he decided to run away. Where or how he could go he did not know; for he had no friends in France who would help him along, and he had no money in his pocket to enable him to help himself.

"I will run away to sea," he said. For the sea, you know, is the first thought of boys who determine to be runaways.

But Napoleon had a strong love for his family; he held high notions in regard to the honor of the family name; above all else, he was determined to do something that should help his family out of its sore straits, and become one element of its support.

"If I should run away to sea," he thought, "I should bring discredit and shame to my family: I should annoy my father, and seriously interfere with my own plans. For, should I run away from Brienne, my father, who has been at such pains to place me here, would be distressed, and perhaps injured. No; I will brave it out. But I will write to my father, asking him to take me away, and place me in some school where I shall feel less like an outcast, where poverty would not be held as a crime, and where I shall have more agreeable surroundings. So he went into his garden fortress; he stretched himself at full length on his bench, and, using the cover of his favorite book, Plutarch's "Lives," as a desk, he wrote this letter to his father: -

"MY FATHER, - If you or my protectors cannot give me the means of sustaining myself more honorably in the house where I am, please summon me home, and as soon as possible. I am tired of poverty, and of the smiles of the insolent scholars who are superior to me only in their fortune; for there is not one among them who feels one-hundredth part of the noble sentiments by which I am animated. Must your son, sir, continually be the butt of these boobies, who, vain of the luxuries which they enjoy, insult me with their laughter at the privations I am forced to endure? No, father; No! If fortune refuses to smile upon me, take me from Brienne, and make me, if you will, a mechanic. From these words you may judge of my despair. This letter, sir, please believe, is not dictated by a vain desire to enjoy expensive amusements. I have no such wish. I feel simply that it is necessary to show my companions that I can procure them as well as they, if I wish to do so.

"Your respectful and affectionate son,
"BONAPARTE."

It took some time to write this letter; for, with Napoleon, letter-writing was always a detested task.

When he had written and directed it, he felt better. We always do feel relieved, you know, if we speak out or write down our feelings. Then he read a chapter in Plutarch about Alexander the Great. This set him to thinking and planning how he would win a battle if he should ever become a leader and commander. He had a notion that he knew just what he would do; and, to prove that his plan was good, he threw himself on the garden walk, and gathering a lot of pebbles, he began to set them in array, as if they were soldiers, and to make all the moves and marches and counter-marches of a furious battle. He indicated the generals and chief officers in this army of stone by the larger pebbles; and you may be sure that the largest pebble of all represented the commander-in-chief - and that was Napoleon himself.

As he marshalled his pebble army, under the lead of his generals and officers, shifting some, advancing others, rearranging certain of them in squares, and massing others as if to resist an attack, Napoleon was conscious of a snickering sort of laugh from somewhere above him.

He looked up, and caught sight of a mocking face looking down at him from the top of the hedge that bordered his garden.

"Ho, ho! Straw-nose!" the spy cried out; "and what is the baby doing? Is it playing with the pretty pebbles? Is it making mud-pies? It was a sweet child, so it was."

Napoleon flushed with anger, enraged both at the intrusion and the teasing.

"Pig! imbecile!" he cried; "get down from my hedge, or I will make you!"

"Ho! hear the infant!" came back the taunting answer. "He will make me - this pretty Corsican baby who plays with pebbles. He will make me! That is good! I laugh; I - Oh, help! help! the Corsican has killed me!"

For a moment Napoleon thought indeed he had; for a moment, too, I am afraid, he did not care. For so enraged was he at the boy's insults and actions, that he had caught up his biggest pebble, which happened to be Napoleon the general, and flung it at the intruder. It struck him squarely between the eyes, and so stunned him that he fell back from the hedge, and lay, first howling, and then terribly quiet, in the space outside Napoleon's garden. At once there was a hue and cry; Napoleon was summoned from his retreat, and dragged before his teacher.

"Ah, miserable one!" cried the master. "And is it you again? You have perhaps killed your fellow-student. You will yet end in the Bastille, or on the block. Take him away, until we see what shall be the result of the last ill-doing of this wicked one."

"When one plays the spy and the bully one must expect retribution," said Napoleon loftily. "This Bouquet is a rascal who will be more likely to end in the Bastille than I, who did but defend my own."

This language, of course, did not help matters; so into the school-cage, or punishment "lock-up" for the school-boy offenders, young Napoleon was at once hurried, without an opportunity for explanation or protest.

CHAPTER ELEVEN.

FRIENDS AND FOES.

Napoleon, the prisoner in the school "lock-up," raged for a while like a caged lion. Then he calmed down into the sulks, returned to his determination to run away, concluded again that he would go to sea, thought of his family and his duties once more, and at last concluded to take his punishment without a word, though he knew that the boy who had mocked him into anger deserved the punishment fully as much as did he who had been the insulted one.

"But then," he reasoned, "he paid well for his taunts and teasing. I wonder how he is now?"

His schoolmate, the English boy, Lawley, was on duty outside the "lock-up" door, as a sort of monitor.

"Say, you Lawley!" Napoleon called out, "and how is that brute of a Bouquet?"

"None the better for seeing you, little one," replied the good-natured English boy, who had that love of fair play that is supposed to belong to all Englishmen, and, therefore, felt that young Bonaparte was suffering unjustly. Then he added:

"Bouquet will no doubt die, and then what will you do?"

"I will plead self-defence, my friend," said Napoleon. "Did not you tell me that an English judge did once declare that a man's home was his castle, which he was pledged to defend from invasion and assault. What else is my garden? That brute of a Bouquet came spying about my castle, and I did but defend myself. Is it not so?"

"It may be so to you, young Bonaparte," Lawley replied; "but not to your judges. No, little one, you're in for it now; they'll make you smart for this, whatever happens to old Bouquet."

For, like all English boys, this young Lawley mingled with his love of justice an equal love for teasing: and like most of the boys at Brienne school, he declared it to be "great fun to get the little Corsican mad."

"Then must you help me to get away from here," Napoleon declared. "Look you, Lawley!" and the boy in great secrecy pulled a paper from his pocket; "see now what I have written."

The English boy took the paper, ran his eye over it, and laughed as loudly as he dared while on duty.

"My eye!" he said, "it's in English, and pretty fair English too. A letter to the British Admiralty? Permission to enter the British navy as a midshipman, eh? Well, you Bonaparte, you are a cool one. A Frenchman in the British navy! Fancy now!"

"No, sir; a Corsican," replied Napoleon. "Why should

it not be so? What have I received but scorn and insult from these Frenchmen? You English are more fair, and England is the friend of Corsica. Why should I not become a midshipman in your navy? The only difficulty, I am afraid, will be my religion."

"Your religion!" cried Lawley, with a laugh; "why, you young rascal! I don't believe you have any religion at all."

"But my family have," Napoleon protested. "My mother's race, the Ramolini" (and the boy rolled out the name as if that respectable farmer family were dukes or emperors at least), "are very strict. I should be disinherited if I showed any signs of becoming a heretic like you English; and if I joined the British navy, would I not be compelled to become a heretic, like you, Lawley?"

Lawley burst into such a loud laugh over the boy's religious scruples, of which he had never before seen evidence, that he aroused one of the teachers with his noise, and had to scud away, for fear of being caught, and punished for neglect of duty.

But he kept Napoleon's letter of application. He must have sent it, either in fun, or with some desire to befriend this badgered Corsican boy; for to-day Napoleon's letter still exists in the crowded English department, wherein are filed the archives of the British Admiralty.

At last, by the interest of certain of the friends whom the boy's misfortune, if not his pluck, had made for him - such lads as Lawley, the English boy, Bourrienne, Lauriston, and Father Patrault, the teacher of mathematics, - Napoleon was liberated with a reprimand; while the boy who had caused all the trouble went unpunished, save for the headache that Napoleon's well-aimed stone had given him and the scar the blow had left.

But the boy could not long stay out of trouble. The next time it came about, friendship, and not vindictiveness, was the cause.

Napoleon did not forget the good offices of his friends. Indeed, Napoleon never forgot a benefit. His final fall from his great power came, largely, because of the very men whom he had honored and enriched, out of friendship or appreciation for services performed in his behalf.

One day young Lauriston, who was on duty as a sort of sentry in the chestnut avenue that was one of Napoleon's favorite walks, left his post, and joining Napoleon, begged him to help him in a problem in mathematics which he had been too lazy or too stupid to solve.

"We will go to your garden, Straw-nose," said Lauriston; for both friend and foe, after the manner of boys, used the nicknames that had by common consent been fastened upon their schoolfellows.

"We will not, then," Napoleon returned. For, as you know, his garden was sacred, and not even his friends were allowed entrance. "See, we will go beyond, to the seat under the big chestnut. But are you not on duty here?"

Lauriston snapped his fingers and shrugged his

shoulders in contempt of duty. "That for duty!" he exclaimed. "My duty now is to get out this pig of a problem."

Under the big chestnut, which was another of Napoleon's favorite resorts, the two boys put their heads together over Lauriston's problem, and it was soon made clear to the lad; for Napoleon was always good at mathematics.

But the time spent over the problem exhausted Lauriston's limit of duty; and when the teacher came to relieve him at his post, the boy was nowhere to be seen.

Now, at Brienne, military instruction was on military rules; and no crime against military discipline is much greater than "absence without leave."

So when, at last, young Lauriston was found in Napoleon's company, away from his post of duty, and beneath the big chestnut-tree, the boy was in a "pretty mess." But Napoleon never deserted his friends.

"Sir," he said to the teacher, "the fault is mine. I led young Lauriston away to" - he stopped: it would scarcely help his friend's cause to say that he had been helping him at his lessons; thus he continued, "to show him my lists" - which was not an untruth, for he had shown the copy to Lauriston.

"Your lists, unruly one," said the teacher - one of Napoleon's chief persecutors. "And what lists, pray?"

"My lists of the possessions of England, here in my copy-book," said Napoleon, drawing the badly scrawled blank-book from his pocket.

He handed it to the teacher.

"Ah, what handwriting! It is vilely done, young Bonaparte. Even I can scarcely read it," he said. "What is this? You would draw my portrait in your copy-book? Wretched one! have you no manners? So! Possessions of the English, is it? Would that the English possessed you! None then would be happier than I." Thereupon the teacher read through the list, making sarcastic comments on each entry, until he came to the end. "'Cabo Corso in Guinea, a pretty strong fort on the sea side of Fort Royal, a defence of sixteen cannons.' Bad spelling, worse writing, this! and the last, 'Saint Helena, a little island;' and where might it be, that Saint Helena, young Bonaparte?"

"In the South Atlantic, well off the African coast," replied Napoleon.

"Would you were there too, young malcontent!" said the teacher, "luring boys from their duty. This is worse than treason. See! you shall to the lockup once more. And you are no longer battalion captain."

Young Lauriston would have protested against this injustice, and declared that he was at fault; but, like too many boys under similar circumstances, he was afraid, and accepted anything that should save him from punishment. Moreover, a glance at Napoleon's masterful eyes held his tongue mute, and he saw his friend borne away to the punishment that should have been his.

"'Tis Saint Helena's fault, and not yours, my

Lauriston," Napoleon whispered in his ear. "Bad writing is never forgiven."

So, as if in a prophecy of the future, Napoleon suffered unjust disgrace in connection with Saint Helena's name; and to-day, in the splendid exhibition-room of the historical library at Florence, jealously guarded beneath a glass case, is Napoleon's blue paper copy-book, the very last line of which reads, by the strangest of all strange coincidences, "Saint Helena, a little island."

The boy's willingness to suffer for his friends, and, even more than this, the unjust taking away of his office in the school battalion, of which he was quite proud, turned the tide in young Napoleon's favor, so far as his schoolmates were concerned.

"Little Straw-nose is a plucky one, is he not, though?" the boys declared; and when he came on the field again, they welcomed him with cheers, and made him leader for the day in their sports.

They had great fun. Napoleon, full of his readings in Plutarch's "Lives," divided the boys into two camps; one camp was to be the Persians, the other the Greeks and Macedonians. Napoleon, of course, was Alexander; and, like the great Macedonian, he wrought such havoc on the Persians, that the school hall in which the battle was waged was filled with the uproar, and all the teachers at Brienne rushed pell-mell to the place, to quell what they were certain must be a school riot, led on by "that miserable Corsican."

Day by day, however, "that miserable Corsican" made more and more friends among his schoolfellows. For boys grow tired at last of plaguing one who has both spirit and pluck; and these Napoleon certainly possessed. He had come to the school "a little savage," so the polished French boys declared.

"I was in Brienne," he said years afterwards, as he thought over his school-days, "the poorest of all my schoolfellows. They always had money in their pockets; I, never. I was proud, and was most careful that nobody should perceive this. I could neither laugh nor amuse myself like the others. I was not one of them. I could not be popular."

So he had to go through the same hard training that other poor boys at boarding-school have undergone. He, however was petulant, high-spirited, proud, and had something of that Corsican love of retaliation that has made that rocky island famous for its feuds and family rows, or "vendettas" as they are called.

He showed the boys at last that they could not impose upon him; that he had plenty of spirit; that he was kind-hearted to those who showed themselves friendly; and, above all, that he was fitted to lead them in their sports, and could, in fact, help them toward having a jolly good time.

So, gradually, they began to side with and follow him. They left him in undisturbed possession of his fortified garden, they asked his help over hard points in mathematics, until at last he began even to grow a little popular. And then, to crown all, came the great Snowball Fight.

CHAPTER TWELVE.

THE GREAT SNOW-BALL FIGHT
AT BRIENNE SCHOOL.

That Snow-ball Fight is now famous. It was in the winter of 1783. Snow fell heavily; drifts piled up in the schoolyard at Brienne. The schoolboys marvelled and exclaimed; for such a snow-fall was rare in France. Then they began to shiver and grumble. They shivered at the cold, to which they were not accustomed; they grumbled at the snow which, by covering their playground, kept them from their usual out-of-door sports, and held them for a time prisoners within the dark schoolrooms.

Suddenly Napoleon had an inspiration.

"What is snow for, my brothers," he exclaimed, "if not to be used? Let us use it. What say you to a snow fort and a siege? Who will join me?"

It was a novel idea; and, with all the boyish love for something new and exciting, the boys of Brienne entered into the plan at once. "The fort, the fort, young Straw-nose!" they cried. "Show us what to do! Let us build it at once!"

With Napoleon as director, they straightway set to

work. The boy had an excellent head for such things; and his mathematical knowledge, together with the preparatory study in fortifications he had already pursued in the school, did him good service.

He was not satisfied with simply piling up mounds of snow. He built regular works on a scientific plan. The snow "packed well," and the boys worked like beavers. With spades and brooms and hands and homemade wooden shovels, they built under Napoleon's directions a snow fort that set all Brienne wondering and admiring. There were intrenchments and redoubts, bastions and ramparts, and all the parts and divisions and defences that make up a real fort.

It took some days to build this wonderful fort. For the boys could only work in their hours of recess. But at last, when all was ready, Napoleon divided the schoolboys into two unequal portions. The smaller number was to hold the fort as defenders; the larger number was to form the besieging force. At the head of the besiegers was Napoleon. Who was captain of the fort I do not know. His name has not come down to us.

But the story of the Snow-ball Fight has. For days the battle raged. At every recess hour the forces gathered for the exciting sport. The rule was that when once the fort was captured, the besiegers were to become its possessors, and were, in turn, to defend it from its late occupants, who were now the attacking army, increased to the required number by certain of the less skilful fighters in the successful army.

Napoleon was in his element. He was an impetuous leader; but he was skilful too; he never lost his head.

Again and again, as leader of the storming-party, he would direct the attack; and at just the right moment, in the face of a shower of snow-balls, he would dash from his post of observation, head the assaulting army, and scaling the walls with the fire of victory in his eye and the shout of encouragement on his lips, would lead his soldiers over the ramparts, and with a last dash drive the defeated defenders out from the fortification.

The snow held for nearly ten days; the fight kept up as long as the snow walls, often repaired and strengthened, would hold together.

The thaw, that relentless enemy of all snow sports, came to the attack at last, and gradually dismantled the fortifications; snow for ammunition grew thin and poor, and gravel became more and more a part of the snow-ball manufacture.

Napoleon tried to prevent this, for he knew the danger from such missiles. But often, in the heat of battle, his commands were disregarded. One boy especially - the same Bouquet who had scaled his hedge and brought him into trouble - was careless or vindictive in this matter.

On the last day of the snow, Napoleon saw young Bouquet packing snow-balls with dirt and gravel, and commanded him to stop. But Bouquet only flung out a hot "I won't!" at the commander, and launched his gravel snow-ball against the decaying fort.

Napoleon was just about to head the grand assault. "To the rear with you! to the rear, Bouquet! You are disqualified!" he cried.

But Bouquet was insubordinate. He did not intend to be cheated out of his fun by any orders that "Straw-nose" should give him. Instead of obeying his commander, he sang out a contemptuous refusal, and dashed ahead, as if to supplant his general in the post of leader of the assault.

Napoleon had no patience with disobedience. The insubordination and insolence of Bouquet angered him; and darting forward, he collared his rebellious subordinate, and flung him backward down the slushy rampart.

"Imbecile!" he cried. "Learn to obey! Drag him to the rear, Lauriston."

The fort was carried. But "General Thaw" was too strong for the young soldiers; and that night, a rain setting in, finished the destruction of the now historic snow-fort of Brienne School.

Bouquet, smarting under what he considered the disgrace that had been put upon him before his playmates, accosted Napoleon that night in the hall. "Bah, then, smarty Straw-nose!" he cried; "you are a beast. How dare you lay hands on me, a Frenchman?"

"Because you would not obey orders," Napoleon replied. "Was not I in command?"

"You!" sneered Bouquet; "and who are you to command? A runaway Corsican, a brigand, and the son of a brigand, like all Corsicans."

"My father is not a brigand," returned Napoleon. "He is a gentleman - which you are not."

"I am no gentleman, say you?" cried the enraged French boy. "Why, young Straw-nose, my ancestors were gentlemen under great King Louis when yours were tending sheep on your Corsican hills. My father is an officer of France; yours is" -

"Well, sir, and what is mine?" said Napoleon defiantly.

"Yours," Bouquet laughed with a mocking and cruel sneer, "yours is but a lackey, a beggar in livery, a miserable tip-staff!"

Napoleon flung himself at the insulter of his father in a fury; but he was caught back by those standing by, and saved from the disgrace of again breaking the rules by fighting in the school-hall.

All night, however, he brooded over Bouquet's taunting words, and the desire for revenge grew hot within him.

The boy had said his father was no gentleman. No gentleman, indeed! Bouquet should see that he knew how gentlemen should act. He would not fall upon him, and beat him as he deserved. He would conduct himself as all gentlemen did. He would challenge to a duel the insulter of his father.

This was the custom. The refuge of all gentlemen who felt themselves insulted, disgraced, or persecuted in those days, was to seek vengeance in a personal encounter with deadly weapons, called a duel. It is a foolish and savage way of seeking redress; but even today it is resorted to by those who feel themselves ill treated by their "equals." So Napoleon felt that he was doing the only wise and gentlemanly thing possible.

But, even then duelling was against the law. It was punished when men were caught at it; for schoolboys, it was considered an unheard-of crime.

Still, though against the law, all men felt that it was the only way to salve their wounded honor. Napoleon felt it would be the only manly course open to him; so, early next morning, he despatched his friend Bourrienne with a note to Bouquet. That note was a "cartel," or challenge. It demanded that Mr. Bouquet should meet Mr. Bonaparte at such time and place as their seconds might select, there to fight with swords until the insult that Mr. Bouquet had put upon Mr. Bonaparte should be wiped out in blood.

There was ferocity for you! But it was the fashion.

"Mr. Bouquet," however, had no desire to meet the fiery young Corsican at swords' points. So, instead of meeting his adversary, he sneaked off to one of the teachers, who, as we know, most disliked Napoleon, and complained that the Corsican, Bonaparte, was seeking his life, and meant to kill him.

At once Napoleon was summoned before the indignant instructor.

"So, sir!" cried the teacher, "is this the way you seek to become a gentleman and officer of your king? You would murder a schoolmate; you would force him to a duel! No denial, sir; no explanation. Is this so, or not so?"

Once more Napoleon saw that words or remonstrances would be in vain.

"It is so," he replied. "Can we, then, never work out your Corsican brutality?" said the teacher. "Go, sir! you are to be imprisoned until fitting sentence for your crime can be considered."

And once again poor Napoleon went into the school lock-up, while Bouquet, who was the most at fault, went free.

There was almost a rebellion in school over the imprisonment of the successful general who had so bravely fought the battles of the snow-fort.

Napoleon passed a day in the lock-up; then he was again summoned before the teacher who had thus punished him.

"You are an incorrigible, young Bonaparte," said the teacher. "Imprisonment can never cure you. Through it, too, you go free from your studies and tasks. I have considered the proper punishment. It is this: you are to put on to-day the penitent's woollen gown; you are to kneel during dinner-time at the door of the dining-room, where all may see your disgrace and take warning therefrom; you are to eat your dinner on your knees. Thereafter, in presence of your schoolmates assembled in the dining-room, you are to apologize to Mr. Bouquet, and ask pardon from me, as representing the school, for thus breaking the laws and acting as a bully and a murderer. Go, sir, to your room, and assume the penitent's gown."

Napoleon, as I have told you, was a high-spirited boy, and keenly felt disgrace. This sentence was as humiliating and mortifying as anything that could be put upon him. Rebel at it as he might, he knew that he would be forced to do it; and, distressed beyond measure at thought of what he must go through, he sought his room, and flung himself on his bed in an agony of tears. He actually had what in these days we call a fit of hysterics.

While thus "broken up," his room door opened. Supposing that the teacher, or one of the monitors, had come to prepare him for the dreadful sentence, he refused to move.

Then a voice, that certainly was not the one he expected, called to him. He raised a flushed and tearful face from the bed, and met the inquiring eyes of his father's old friend, and the "protector" of the Bonaparte family, General Marbeuf, formerly the French commander in Corsica.

"Why, Napoleon, boy! what does all this mean?" inquired the general. "Have you been in mischief? What is the trouble?"

The visit came as a climax to a most exciting event. In it Napoleon saw escape from the disgrace he so feared, and the injustice against which he so rebelled. With a joyful shout he flung himself impulsively at his friend's feet, clasped his knees, and begged for his protection. The boy, you see, was still unnerved and over-wrought, and was not as cool or self-possessed as usual.

Gradually, however, he calmed down, and told General Marbeuf the whole story.

The general was indignant at the sentence. But he laughed heartily at the idea of this fourteen-year-old boy challenging another to a duel.

"Why, what a fire-eater it is!" he cried. "But you had provocation, boy. This Bouquet is a sneak, and your teacher is a tyrant. But we will change it all; see, now! I will seek out the principal. I will explain it all. He shall see it rightly, and you shall not be thus disgraced. No, sir! not if I, General Marbeuf, intrench myself alone with you behind what is left of your slushy snow-fort yonder, and fight all Brienne school in your behalf - teachers and all. So cheer up, lad! We will make it right."

CHAPTER THIRTEEN.

RECOMMENDED FOR PROMOTION.

General Marbeuf did make it all right. Bouquet was called to account; the teacher who had so often made it unpleasant for Napoleon was sharply reprimanded; and the principal, having his attention drawn to the persistent persecution of this boy from Corsica, consented to his release from imprisonment, while sternly lecturing him on the sin of duelling.

The general also chimed in with the principal's lecture; although I am afraid, being a soldier, he was more in sympathy with Napoleon than he should have been.

"A bad business this duelling, my son," he said, "a bad business - though I must say this rascal Bouquet deserved a good beating for his insolence. But a beating is hardly the thing between gentlemen."

"And you have fought a duel, my General?" inquired Napoleon. "Have I? why, scores" the bluff soldier admitted.

"Let me see - I have fought one - two - four - why, when I was scarcely more than your age, my friend, I" - and then the general suddenly stopped. For he saw how his reminiscences would grow into admissions that would scarcely be a correction.

So, with a hem and a haw, General Marbeuf wisely changed the subject, and began to inquire into the reasons for Napoleon's unpleasant experiences at Brienne. He speedily discovered that the cause lay in the pocket. As you have already learned from Napoleon's letter to his father and his own later reflections, the boy's poverty made him dissatisfied with his lot, while his companions, heedless and blundering as boys are apt to be in such matters, did not try to smooth over the difference between their plenty and this boy's need, but rather increased his bitterness by their thoughtless speech and action.

"Brains do not lie in the pocket, Napoleon, boy," he said. "You have as much intelligence as any of your fellows, you should not be so touchy because you do not happen to have their spending-money. You must learn to be more charitable. Do not take offence so easily; remember that all boys admire ability, and look kindly on good fellowship in a comrade, whether he have much or little in his purse. Learn to be more companionable; accept things as they come; and if you are ever hard pushed for money, - call on me. I'll see you through."

Any boy will take a lecture with so agreeable an ending, and Napoleon did not resent his good friend's advice.

The general also introduced the boy to the great lady who lived in the big chateau near by - the Lady of Brienne. She interested herself in the lad's doings, gave him many a "tip," invited him to her home, and, by kindly words and motherly deeds, brought the boy out of his nervousness and solitude into something more like good manners and gentlemanly ways.

So the school - life at Brienne went on more agreeably as the months passed by. Napoleon studied hard. He made good progress in mathematics and history, though he disliked the languages, and never wrote a good hand. He was always an "old boy" for his years; and, in time, many of his teachers became interested in him, and even grew fond of him.

But he always kept his family in mind. He was continually planning how he might help his mother, and give his brothers and sisters a chance to get an education.

He even treated Joseph as if he himself were the elder, and Joseph the younger brother. There is a letter in existence which he wrote to his father in 1783, in which he tries to arrange for Joseph's future, as that rather heavy boy had decided not to become a priest.

"Joseph," so Napoleon wrote from Brienne to his father, "can come here to school. The principal says he can be received here; and Father Patrault, the teacher of mathematics, says he will be glad to undertake Joseph's instruction, and that, if he will work, we may both of us go together for our artillery examination. Never mind me. I can get along. But you must do something for Joseph. Good-by, my dear father. I hope you will decide to send Joseph here to Brienne, rather than to Metz. It will be a pleasure for us to be together; and, as Joseph knows nothing of mathematics, if you send him to Metz, he will have to begin with the little children; and that, I know, will disgust him. I hope, therefore, that before the end of October I shall embrace Joseph."

That is a nice, brotherly letter, is it not? It does not sound like the boy who was always ready to quarrel and fight with brother Joseph, nor does it seem to be from a sulky, disagreeable boy. This spirit of looking out for his family was one of the traits of Napoleon's character that was noticeable alike in the boy, the soldier, the commander, and the emperor.

Indeed, the very spirit of self-denial in which this letter, an extract from which you have just read, was written, was not only characteristic of this remarkable man of whose boy-life this story tells, but it led in his school-days at Brienne to a change that affected his whole life.

One day there came to the school the Chevalier de Keralio, inspector of military schools - a sort of committee man as you would say in America. It was the duty of the inspector to look into the record, and arrange for the promotions, of "the king's wards," as the boys and girls were called who were educated at the expense of the state. He was, in some way, attracted to this sober, silent, and sad-eyed little Corsican, and inquired into his history. He rather liked the boy's appearance, odd as it was. He took quite a fancy to the young Napoleon, talked with him, questioned him, and outlined to the teachers at Brienne what he thought should be the future course of the lad.

Charles Bonaparte had some thought of placing Napoleon in the naval service of France. The boy told Inspector Keralio this; but the chevalier declared that he intended to recommend the boy for promotion to the military school at Paris, and then have him assigned for service at Toulon. This was the nearest port to Corsica, and would place Napoleon nearer to his much-loved family home.

The teachers objected to this.

"There are other boys in the school much better fitted for such an honor than this young Bonaparte," they said.

But the inspector thought otherwise.

"I know boys," he said. "I know what I am doing."

"But he is not ready yet," said the principal. "To do as you advise would be to change all the rules set down for promotion."

"Well, what if it does?" replied the inspector.

"But why should you favor this boy and his family? They are Corsicans."

"I do not care anything about his family," the inspector declared. "If I put aside the rules in this case, it is not to do the Bonaparte family a favor. I do not know them. But I have studied this boy. It is because of him that I propose this action. I see a spark in him that cannot be too early cultivated. It shall not be extinguished if I can help it. This young Bonaparte will make his mark if he has a chance, and I shall give him that chance."

So before he left Brienne the inspector wrote this strong recommendation of the boy whom he desired to befriend and put forward: -

"Monsieur de Bonaparte (Napoleon), born August 15, 1769. Height, four feet, ten inches. Of good constitution, excellent health, mild disposition. Has finished the fourth form: is straightforward and obliging. His conduct has been most satisfactory. He has been distinguished for his application to mathematics; is fairly acquainted with history and geography; is weak in all accomplishments, - drawing, dancing, music, and the like. This boy would make an excellent sailor. He deserves promotion to the school in Paris."

Napoleon had gained a powerful friend. His favor would put the boy well forward in his career. He felt quite elated. But, unfortunately for the plans proposed, the Inspector de Keralio died suddenly, before his recommendation could be acted upon; and with so many other applications that were backed up by influence, for boys with better opportunities, Napoleon's desired assignment to the naval service did not receive action by the government, and he was passed by in favor of less able but better befriended boys.

So, when the examination - days came, the new Inspector, who came in place of the lad's friend Chevalier de Keralio, decided that young Napoleon Bonaparte was fitted for the artillery service; and at the age of fifteen the boy left the school at Brienne, and was ordered to enter upon a higher course of study at the military school at Paris. Nothing more was said about preparing him for the naval service, for which Inspector de Keralio had recommended him. And in the certificate which he carried from Brienne to Paris, Napoleon was described as a "masterful, impetuous and headstrong boy." Evidently the opinion of Napoleon's teachers was adopted, rather than the prophetic report of his dead friend, Inspector de Keralio.

In after-years Napoleon forgot all the worries and troubles of his school-days at Brienne, and remembered only the pleasant times there.

Once, when he was a man, he heard some bells chiming musically. He stopped, listened, and said to his old schoolmate, whom he had made his secretary, -

"Ah, Bourrienne! that reminds me of my first years at Brienne; we were happy there, were we not?"

To the chaplain who had prepared him for that most important occasion in the lives of all French children, his first communion, and who had taken a fatherly interest in him, Napoleon, when powerful and great, wrote: "I can never forget that to your virtuous example and wise lessons I am indebted for the great fortune that has come to me. Without religion, no happiness, no future, is possible. My dear friend, remember me in your prayers."

Even his old adversary, Bouquet, whose mean ways had brought Napoleon into so many scrapes, was not forgotten. Bouquet was a bad fellow. Years after, he was caught doing some great mischief; and Napoleon, as his superior officer, would have been obliged to punish him. But when he heard that Bouquet had escaped from prison, he really felt relieved.

"Bouquet was my old schoolfellow at Brienne," he said. "I am glad I did not have to punish him."

Whenever he had the chance, after he had risen to

honor and power, he would do his old schoolmates and teachers at Brienne school a service. Bourrienne and Lauriston were both advanced and honored. To one teacher he gave the post of palace librarian; another was appointed the head of the School of Fine Arts; Father Patrault, who had been his friend and had taught him mathematics, was made one of his secretaries; other teachers he helped with pensions or positions; and even the porter of the school was made porter of one of the palaces when Napoleon became an emperor.

At last, as I have told you, when the opportunity came, Napoleon said good-by to Brienne school. He left before his time was up, in order to give his younger brother, Lucien, the chance for a scholarship in the school; he put aside with regret, but without complaining, the wished-for assignment to the naval service. He decided to become an artillery officer; and on October 17, in the year 1784, he started for Paris to enter upon his "king's scholarship" in the military school. He had been a schoolboy at Brienne five years and a half. He was now a boy of fifteen.

CHAPTER FOURTEEN.

NAPOLEON GOES TO PARIS.

Some boys at fifteen are older than other boys at fifteen. Napoleon, as I have told you, was always an "old boy." So when, on that October day in 1784, he arrived at the capital to enter upon the king's scholarship which he had received, he was no longer a child, even though under-sized and somewhat "spindling."

Here, however, as at Autun and Brienne, his appearance was against him, and created an unfavorable impression.

As he got out of the Brienne coach, he ran almost into the arms of one of the boys he had known at Corsica - young Demetrius Compeno.

"What, Demetrius! you here?" he cried, a smile of pleasure at sight of a familiar face lighting up his sallow features.

"And why not, young Bonaparte," Demetrius laughed back in reply. "You did not suppose I was going to let you fall right into the lion's mouth, undefended. Why, you are so fresh and green looking, the beast would take you for Corsican grass, and eat you at once."

Although Napoleon was inclined to resent this pleasantry, he was too delighted to meet an old friend to say much. And, the truth is, the great city did surprise him. For, even though he had been five years at Brienne school, he was still a country boy, and walked the streets gaping and staring at everything he saw, like a boy at his first circus.

"Why, boy! if I were not with you," said Demetrius, with the superior air of the boy who knows city ways, "I don't know what snare you would not fall into. While you were staring at the City Hall, or the Soldier's Home, or that big statue of King Henry on the bridge, one of those street-boys who is laughing at you yonder would have picked your pockets, snatched your satchel, or perhaps (who knows?) cut your throat. Oh, yes! they do such things in Paris. You must learn to look out for yourself here."

"I think I am big enough for that," cried Napoleon.

"You big! why, you are but a child, young Bonaparte!" Demetrius exclaimed. "But we'll make a man of you at the Paris school."

The boys at the Paris Military School - the West Point of France in those days - proceeded at once to try to "make a man" of Napoleon in the same way that all boys seem ever ready to do; as, indeed, the boys at Autun and Brienne had done - by poking fun at the new cadet, mimicking his manners, ridiculing his appearance, and making life generally unpleasant.

But Napoleon had learned one thing by his bitter experiences at the other schools he had attended, - he had learned to control his temper, and take things as they came, with less of revenge and sullenness. The kindly criticism of his friends, General Marbeuf and Inspector de Keralio, had left their effect upon him; and besides the companionship of his fellow-countryman, Demetrius Comneno, he had the good fortune to make his first really boy-friend in his roommate at the military school. This was young Alexander des Mazes, a fine lad of his own age, "a noble by birth and nature," who conceived a liking for Napoleon at once, and was his friend for many years.

In Paris, too, he had the advantage of the friendship of a fine Corsican family, - the Permous, relatives of Demetrius, and old acquaintances of the Bonaparte family. His sister Eliza was also at school at the girls' academy of St. Cyr; and Napoleon visited her frequently, and talked over home matters and other mutual interests. For Napoleon had long since forgiven and forgotten the trouble into which Eliza had once plunged him because of her love for the fruit of their uncle, the canon; and the brother and sister could now laugh over that childish experience, while Eliza dearly loved Napoleon, in spite of her selfishness, and even because of his so uncomplainingly bearing her punishment.

Napoleon, though "an odd child," as people called him, was wide awake and critical. He observed everything, and thought much. He was not long in noticing one thing: that was, the recklessness, the extravagance, and the indifference of the boys who were being educated at the king's expense in the king's military school.

Most of these boys were of high birth, accustomed to having their own way, and with extravagant tastes and notions. Napoleon spoke of this frequently to the friends he made; but both Demetrius and Alexander laughed at him, and said, "Well, what of it? Would you have us all digs and hermits - like you? Here is the chance to have a good time, to live high, and to let the king pay for it - the king or our fathers. Why shouldn't we do as we please?"

"But, Demetrius!" Napoleon protested, "that is not the way to make soldiers. Do you think those fellows will be good officers, if they never know what it is to deny themselves, or to do the work that is their duty, but which they leave for servants to do?" For Napoleon, you see, had many of the saving ways of his practical mother, and rebelled at the unconcern of these luxury-loving and careless boys, who were supposed to be learning the discipline of soldiers in their Paris school.

Demetrius only snapped his fingers, as Alexander shrugged his shoulders, in contempt of what they considered Napoleon's countrified way.

But all this show of pomp and luxury really troubled this boy, who had long before learned the value of money and the need of self-denial. Indeed, it worried him so much that one day he sat down and wrote a letter which he intended to send as a protest to the minister of war, actually lecturing that high and mighty officer, and "giving him points" on the proper way to educate boys in the French military schools.

Fortunately for him, he sent the letter first to his old instructor, the principal of the Brienne school. And the instructor - even though he, perhaps, agreed with this boy-critic - saw how foolish and hurtful for Napoleon's interest it would be to send such a surprising letter; and he promptly suppressed it. But the letter still exists;

and a curious epistle it is for a fifteen-year-old boy to write. Here is a part of it:

"The king's scholars," so Napoleon wrote to the minister, "could only learn in this school, in place of qualities of the heart, feelings of vanity and self-satisfaction to such an extent, that, on returning to their own homes, they would be far from sharing gladly in the simple comfort of their families, and would perhaps blush for their fathers and mothers, and despise their modest country surroundings. Instead of maintaining a large staff of servants for these pupils, and giving them every day meals of several courses, and keeping up an expensive stable full of horses and grooms, would it not be better, Mr. Minister - of course without interrupting their studies - to compel them to look after their own wants themselves? That is to say, without compelling them to really do their own cooking, would it not be wise to have them eat soldiers' bread or something no better, to accustom them to beat and brush their own clothes, to clean their own boots and shoes, and do other things equally useful and self-helpful? If they were thus accustomed to a sober life, and to be particular about their appearance, they would become healthier and stronger; they could support with courage the hardships of war, and inspire with respect and blind devotion the soldiers who would have to serve under their orders." How do you think the grand minister of war would have felt to get such a lecturing on discipline from a boy at school? and what do you imagine the boys would have done had they heard that one of their schoolmates had written a letter, suggesting that they be deprived of their pleasures and pamperings? It was lucky for young Napoleon that the principal at Brienne got hold of the letter before it was forwarded to the war minister.

But then, as you have heard before, Napoleon was an odd boy. He thought so himself when he grew to be a man, and he laughed at the recollection of his manners. He laid it all, however, to the responsibility he had felt, even from the day when he was a little fellow, because of the needs of his hard-pushed family in Corsica. "All these cares," he once said, looking back over his boy-life, "spoiled my early years; they influenced my temper, and made me grave before my time."

Even if he did not send that critical and most unwise letter for a boy of his standing, the insight he gained into the expensive ways of the pupils at the military school had its effect upon him; and the very criticisms of that remarkable letter were used for their original purpose when Napoleon came to authority and power. For, when he was emperor of France, he gave to the minister who had the military schools in charge this order: "No pupil is to cost the state more than twenty-five cents a day. These pupils are sons either of soldiers or of working-men; it is absolutely contrary to my intention to give them habits of life which can only be hurtful to them."

If Napoleon was so critical as to the ways and style of his schoolmates, he certainly set the lesson in economy for himself that he suggested for them.

To be sure, he had no money to waste or to spend; but he might have been hail-fellow with the other boys, and joined in their luxuries, had he but been willing to borrow, as did the rest of them. But Napoleon had always a horror of debt. He had acquired this from his mother's teachings and his father's spendthrift ways. Even as a boy, however, his will was so strong, his power of self-denial was so great, that he continued in what he considered the path of duty, unmindful of the boyish charges of "mean fellow" and "pauper" that the spoiled spendthrifts of the school had no hesitation in casting at him.

At last, however, these culminated almost in an open row; and Napoleon found himself called upon either to explain his position, or become both unpopular and an "outcast" because of what his schoolmates considered his stinginess and parsimony.

It was this way - But I had better tell you the story in a new chapter.

CHAPTER FIFTEEN.

A TROUBLE OVER POCKET MONEY.

It was the twelfth of June in the year 1785 that a group of scholars was standing, during the recess hour, in a corner of the military school of Paris.

They were all boys; but they assumed the manners and gave themselves the airs of princes of the blood.

"Gentlemen," said one who seemed to be most prominent in the group, "I have called you together on a most important matter. Tomorrow is old Bauer's birthday. I propose that, as is our custom, we take some notice of it. What do you say to giving him a little supper, in the name of the school?"

"A good idea; a capital idea, d'Hebonville!" exclaimed most of the boys, in ready acquiescence.

"A gluttonous idea, I call it; and an expensive one," said one upon the outer edge of the circle, in a sharply critical tone. "Ah. our little joker has a word to say," exclaimed one of the boys sarcastically, drawing back, and pushing the speaker to the front; "hear him."

"Oh, now, Napoleon! don't object," young Alexander des Mazes said. "Did you not hear why d'Hebonville proposed the supper? It is to honor the German teacher's birthday."

"Oh, he heard it fast enough, des Mazes," rejoined d'Hebonville. "That is what makes him so cross."

"Why do you say that?" Napoleon demanded.

"You do not like the plan because it is to honor old Bauer; for you do not like him," d'Hebonville replied. "If, now, it were a supper to the history teacher, you would agree, I am sure. For de l'Equille praises you on 'the profundity of your reflections and the sagacity of your judgment.' Oh, I've read his notes; or you would agree if it were Domaisen, the rhetoric teacher, who is much impressed - those are his very words, are they not, gentlemen? - with 'your powers of generalization, which' he says, are even 'as granite heated at a volcano.' But as it is only dear old Bauer" - and d'Hebonville shrugged his shoulders significantly. "Well, and what about 'dear old Bauer,' as you call him?" cried Napoleon; "finish, sir; finish, I say."

"I will tell you what Father Bauer says of you, Napoleon," said des Mazes laughingly, as he laid his arm familiarly about Napoleon's neck; "he says he does not think much of you, because you make no progress in your German; and as old Bauer thinks the world moves only for Germans, he has nothing good to say of one who makes no mark in his dear language. 'Ach!' says old Bauer, 'your Napoleon Bonaparte will never be anything but a fool. He knows no German.'"

The boys laughed loudly at des Mazes's mimicry of the German teacher's manner and speech. But Napoleon smiled with the air of one who felt himself superior to the teacher of German.

"Now, I should say," said Philip Mabille, "that here is the very reason why Napoleon should not refuse to join us. It will be - what are the words? - 'heaping coals of fire' on old Bauer's head."

"That might be so," Napoleon agreed, in a better humor. "But why give him a feast? Let us - I'll tell you - let us give him a spectacle. A battle, perhaps."

"In which you should be a general, I suppose, as you were in that snow - ball fight at Brienne, of which we have heard once or twice," said d'Hebonville sarcastically.

"And why not?" asked Napoleon haughtily.

"Or the death of Caesar, like the tableaux we arranged at Brienne," suggested Demetrius Comneno enthusiastically.

"In which your great Napoleon played Brutus, I suppose," said d'Hebonville. "No, no; the birthday of old Bauer is not a solemn occasion to demand a battle or a spectacle; something much more simple will do for a professor of German. Let us make it a good collation. There are fifteen of us in his class. If each one of us contributes five dollars, we could get up quite a feast."

"Oh, see here, d'Hebonville!" cried Mabille; "think a little. Five dollars is a good deal for some of us. Not all of the fifteen can afford so much. I don't believe I could; nor you, Napoleon, could you?" Napoleon's face grew sober, but he said nothing.

"Oh, well! let only those pay then who can," said d'Hebonville.

"Who, then, will take part in your feast?" demanded Napoleon.

"Why, all of us, of course," replied d'Hebonville.

"At the feast, or in giving the money," queried Mabille.

"At the feast, to be sure," d'Hebonville answered.

"Come, now; we should have no feeling in this matter," cried des Mazes. "We will decide for you, Mabille."

"Old Bauer must not dream that there are any of his class who do not share in the matter," said Comneno. "That would be showing a preference, and a preference is never fair."

"And do you wish, then," said Mabille, "that old Bauer should be under obligation to me, for example, who can pay little or nothing toward the feast?"

"Certainly; to you as much as to the richest among us," said d'Hebonville.

"Bah!" cried Napoleon. "That would imply a sentiment of gratitude toward my masters; and I, for one, have none to this Professor Bauer."

"Some one to see Napoleon Bonaparte," said a porter of the school, appearing at the door of the schoolroom. "He waits in the parlor."

Without a word Napoleon left his school-fellows; but they looked after him with faces expressive of disapproval or disappointment.

The disagreeable impression produced by the discussion in which he had been taking part still remained with Napoleon as he entered the parlor to meet his visitor. It was the friend of his family, Monsieur de Permon.

Napoleon, indeed, was scarce able to greet his visitor pleasantly. But Monsieur de Permon, without appearing to notice the boy's ill-humor, greeted him pleasantly, and said, -

"Madame de Permon and I are on our way to the Academy of St. Cyr, to see your sister Eliza. Would you not like to go with us, Napoleon? I have permission for you to be absent"

Napoleon brightened at this invitation, and gladly accepted it. The two proceeded to the carriage, in which Madame Permon was awaiting them; and the three were soon on the road to the school of St. Cyr, in which, as I have told you, Eliza Bonaparte was a scholar.

They were ushered into the parlor, and Eliza was summoned. She soon appeared; but she entered the room slowly and disconsolately; her eyes were red with crying. Eliza was evidently in trouble.

"Why, Eliza, my dear child, what is the matter?" Madame Permon exclaimed, drawing the girl toward her. "You have been crying. Have they been scolding you here?"

"No, madame," Eliza replied in a low tone.

"Are you afraid they may? Have you trouble with your lessons?" persisted Madame Permon.

With the same dejected air, Eliza answered as before, "No, madame."

"But what, then, is the matter, my dear?" cried Madame Permon; "such red eyes mean much crying."

Eliza was silent.

"Come, Eliza!" Napoleon demanded with an elder brother's authority; "speak! answer Madame here What is the matter?"

But even to her brother, Eliza made no reply.

Then Madame Permon, as tenderly as if she had been the girl's mother, led her aside; and finding a remote seat in a corner, she drew the child into her lap.

"Eliza," she said with gracious kindliness, "I must know why you are in sorrow. Think of me as your mother, dear; as one who must act in her place until you return to her. Speak to me as to your mother. Let me have your love and confidence. Tell me, my child, what troubles you."

The tender solicitude of her mother's friend quite vanquished Eliza's stubbornness. Her tears burst out afresh; and between the sobs she stammered, -

"You know, Madame, that Lucie de Montluc leaves the school in eight days."

"I did not know it, Eliza," Madame Permon said, keeping back a smile; "but if that so overcomes you, then am I sorry too."

"Oh, no, Madame'" Eliza said, just a bit indignant at being misunderstood; "it is not her leaving that makes me cry; but, you see, on the day she goes away her class will give her a good - by supper."

"What! and you are not invited?" exclaimed Madame Permon. "Ah, that is the trouble, Madame," cried Eliza, the tears gathering again. "I am invited."

"And yet you cry?"

"It is because each girl is to contribute towards the supper; and I, Madame, can give nothing. My allowance is gone."

"So!" Madame Permon whispered, glad to have at last reached the real cause of the trouble, "that is the matter. And you have nothing left?"

"Only a dollar, Madame," replied Eliza. "But if I give that, I shall have no more money; and my allowance does not come to me for six weeks. Indeed, what I have is not enough for my needs until the six weeks are over. Am I not miserable?"

Napoleon, who had gradually drawn nearer the corner, thrust his hand into his pocket as he heard Eliza's complaint. But he drew it out as quickly. His pocket was empty. Mortified and angry, he stamped his foot in despair. But no one noticed this pantomime.

"How much, my dear, is necessary to quiet this great

sorrow?" Madame Permon asked of Eliza with a smile. Eliza looked into her good friend's eyes.

"Oh, Madame! it is an immense sum," she replied,

"Let me know the worst," Madame Permon said, with affected distress. "How much is it?"

"Two dollars!" confessed Eliza in despair.

"Two dollars!" exclaimed Madame Permon; "what extravagant ladies we are at St. Cyr!" Then she hugged Eliza to her; and, as she did so, she slyly slipped a five-dollar piece into the girl's hand. "Hush! take it, and say nothing," she said; for, above all, she did not wish her action to be seen by Napoleon. For Madame Permon well knew the sensitive pride of the Bonaparte children.

Soon after they left the school; and when once they were within the carriage Napoleon's ill-humor burst forth, in spite of himself.

"Was ever anything more humiliating?" he cried; "was ever anything more unjust? See how it is with that poor child. The rich and poor are placed together, and the poor must suffer or be pensioners. Is it not abominable, the way these schools of St. Cyr and the Paris military are run? Two dollars for a scholars' picnic in a place where no child is supposed to have money. It is enormous!"

His friends made no reply to this boyish outburst; but, when the military school was reached, Monsieur Permon followed Napoleon into the parlor.

"Napoleon," he said, "at your age one is not furious against the world unless he has particular reason."

"And are not my sister's tears a reason, sir, when I cannot remedy their cause?" Napoleon answered with emotion.

"But when I came here for you," said Monsieur Permon, "you, too, appeared angry, as if some trouble had occurred between yourself and your schoolfellows."

"I am unfortunate, sir, not to be able to conceal my feelings," said Napoleon; "but it does seem as if the boys here delighted in making me feel my poverty. They live in an insolent luxury; and whoever cannot imitate them," - here Napoleon dashed a hand to his forehead, - "Oh, it is to die of humiliation!"

"At your age, my Napoleon, one submits and blames no one," said Monsieur Permon, smiling, in spite of himself, at the boy's desperation.

"At my age' yes, sir," Napoleon rejoined, as if keeping back some great thought. "But later - ah, if, some day, I should ever be master! However" - and the French shrug that is so eloquent completed the sentence.

"However," - Monsieur Permon took up his words - "while waiting, one may now and then find a friend. And you take your part here with the boys, do you not?"

Napoleon was silent; and Monsieur Permon, remembering the trouble that had weighed Eliza down, concluded also that some such trial might be a part of

Napoleon's school-life.

"Let me help you, my boy," he said.

At this unexpected proposition Napoleon flushed deeply; then the red tinge paled into the sallow one again, and he responded, "I thank you, sir, but I do not need it."

"Napoleon," said Monsieur Permon, "your mother is my wife's dearest friend; your father has long been my good comrade. Is it right for sons to refuse the love of their fathers, or for boys to reject the friendships of their elders? Pride is excellent; but even pride may sometimes be pernicious. It is pride that sets a barrier between you and your companions. Do not permit it. Regard friendship as of more value than self-consideration; and, for my sake, let me help you to join in these occasions that may mean so much to you in the way of friendship."

Thus deftly did good Monseiur Permon smooth over the bitterness that inequality in pocket allowances so often stirs between those who have little and those who have much.

Napoleon fixed upon his father's friend one of his piercing looks, and taking his proffered money, said: -

"I accept it, sir, as if it came from my father, as you wish me to consider it. But if it came as a loan, I could not receive it. My people have too many charges already; and I ought not to increase them by expenses which, as is often the case here, are put upon me by the folly of my schoolfellows."

The Permons proved good friends to the Bonaparte children; and it was to their house at Montpellier that, in the spring of 1785, Charles Bonaparte was brought to die.

For ill health and misfortune proved too much for this disheartened Corsican gentleman; and, before his boys were grown to manhood, he gave up his unsuccessful struggle for place and fortune. He had worked hard to do his best for his boys and girls; he had done much that the world considers unmanly; he had changed and shifted, sought favors from the great and rich, and taken service that he neither loved nor approved. But he had done all this that his children might be advanced in the world; and though he died in debt, leaving his family almost penniless, still he had spent himself in their behalf; and his children loved and honored his memory, and never forgot the struggles their father had made in their behalf. In fact, much of his spirit of family devotion descended to his famous son Napoleon, the schoolboy.

CHAPTER SIXTEEN.

LIEUTENANT PUSS-IN-BOOTS.

Napoleon returned to his studies after his father's death, poorer than ever in pocket, and greatly distressed over his mother's condition.

For Charles Bonaparte's death had taken away from the family its main support. The income of their uncle, the canon, was hardly sufficient for the family's needs. Joseph gave up his endeavors, and returned to Corsica to help his mother. But Napoleon remained at the military school; for his future depended upon his completing his studies, and securing a position in the army.

How much the boy had his mother in his thoughts, you may judge from this letter which he wrote her a month after his father's death:

MY DEAR MOTHER, - Now that time has begun to soften the first transports of my sorrow. I hasten to express to you the gratitude I feel for all the kindness you have always displayed toward us. Console yourself, dear mother, circumstances require that you should. We will redouble our care and our gratitude, happy if, by our obedience, we can make up to you in the smallest degree for the inestimable loss of a cherished husband I finish, dear mother, - my grief compels it - by praying you to calm yours. My health is perfect, and my daily prayer is that Heaven may grant you the same. Convey my respects to my Aunt Gertrude, to Nurse Saveria, and to my Aunt Fesch.

Your very humble and affectionate son,
NAPOLEON.

At the same time he wrote to his kind old uncle, the Canon Lucien, saying: "It would be useless to tell you how deeply I have felt the blow that has just fallen upon us. We have lost a father; and God alone knows what a father, and what were his attachment and devotion to us. Alas! everything taught us to look to him as the support of our youth. But the will of God is unalterable. He alone can console us."

These letters from a boy of sixteen would scarcely give one the idea that Napoleon was the selfish and sullen youth that his enemies are forever picturing; they rather show him as he was, - quiet, reserved, reticent, but with a heart that could feel for others, and a sympathy that strove to lessen, for the mother he loved, the burden of sorrow and of loss.

That the death of his father, and the "hard times" that came upon the Bonapartes through the loss of their chief bread-winner, did sober the boy Napoleon, and made him even more retiring and reserved, there is no doubt. His old friend, General Marbeuf, was no longer in condition to help him; and, indeed, Napoleon's pride would not permit him to receive aid from friends, even when it was forced upon him.

"I am too poor to run into debt," he declared.

So he became again a hermit, as in the early days at Brienne school. He applied himself to his studies, read much, and longed for the day when he should be transferred from the school to the army.

The day came sooner than even he expected. He had scarcely been a year at the Paris school when he was ordered to appear for his final examination. Whether it was because his teachers pitied his poverty, and wished him to have a chance for himself, or whether because, as some would have us believe, they wished to be rid of a scholar who criticized their methods, and was fault-finding, unsocial, and "exasperating," it is at least certain that the boy took his examinations, and passed them satisfactorily, standing number forty in a class of fifty-eight.

"You are a lucky boy, my Napoleon," said his roommate, Alexander des Mazes; "see! you are ahead of me. I am number fifty-six; pretty near to the foot that, eh?"

"Near enough, Alexander," Napoleon replied; "but I love you fifty-six times better than any of the other boys; and what would you have, my friend? Are not we two of the six selected for the artillery? That is some compensation. Now let us apply for an appointment in the same regiment."

They did so, and secured each a lieutenancy in an artillery regiment. This, however, was not hard to secure; for the artillery service was considered the hardest in the army; and the lazy young nobles and gentlemen of the Paris military school had no desire for real work.

The certificate given to Napoleon upon his graduation read thus: - "This young man is reserved and studious, he prefers study to any amusement, and enjoys reading the best authors, applies himself earnestly to the abstract sciences, cares little for anything else. He is silent, and loves solitude. He is capricious, haughty, and excessively egotisical, talks little, but is quick and energetic in his replies, prompt and severe in his repartees, has great pride and ambition, aspiring to any thing. The young man is worthy of patronage."

And upon the margin of the report one of the examining officers wrote this extra indorsement -

"A Corsican by character and by birth. If favored by circumstances, this young man will rise high."

Napoleon's school-life was over. On the first of September, 1785, he received the papers appointing him second-lieutenant in the artillery regiment, named La Fere (or "the sword"), and was ordered to report at the garrison at Valence. His room-mate and friend, Alexander des Mazes, was appointed to the same regiment.

It was a proud day for the boy of sixteen. At last his school-life was at an end. He was to go into the world as a man and a soldier.

I am afraid he did not look very much like a man, even if he felt that he was one. But he put on his uniform of lieutenant, and in high spirits set off to visit his friends, the Permons.

They lived in a house on one of the river streets - Monsieur and Madame Permon, and their two daughters, Cecilia and Laura.

Now, both these daughters were little girls, and as ready to see the funny side of things as little girls usually are.

So when Lieutenant Napoleon Bonaparte, aged sixteen, came into the room, proud of his new uniform, and feeling that he looked very smart, Laura glanced at Cecilia, and Cecilia smiled at Laura, and then both girls began to laugh.

Madam Permon glanced at them reprovingly, while welcoming the young lieutenant with pleasant words.

But the boy felt that the girls were laughing at him, and he turned to look at himself in the mirror to see what was wrong.

Nothing was wrong. It was simply Napoleon; but Napoleon just then was not a handsome boy. Long-haired, large-headed, sallow-faced, stiff-stocked, and feeling very new in his new uniform (which could not be very gorgeous, however, because the boy's pocket would not admit of any extras in the way of adornment on decoration), he was, I expect, rather a pinched-looking, queer-looking boy; and, moreover, his boots were so big, and his legs were so thin, that the legs appeared lost in the boots.

As he glanced at himself in the mirror, the girls giggled again, and their mother said, -

"Silly ones, why do you laugh? Is our new uniform so marvellous a change that you do not recognize Lieutenant Bonaparte?"

"Lieutenant Bonaparte, mamma!" cried fun-loving Laura. "No, no! not that. See! is not Napoleon for all the world like - like Lieutenant Puss-in-Boots?"

Whereupon they laughed yet more merrily, and Napoleon laughed with them.

"My boots are big, indeed," he said; "too big, perhaps; but I hope to grow into them. How was it with Puss-in-Boots, girls? He filled his well at last, did he not? You will be sorry you laughed at me, some day, when I march into your house, a big, fat general. Come, let us go and see Eliza. They may go with me, eh, Madame?"

"Yes; go with the lieutenant, children," said Madame Permon.

So they all went to call on Eliza, at the school of St. Cyr, and you may be sure that she admired her brother, the new lieutenant, boots and all. And as they came home, Napoleon took the little girls into a toy-store, and bought for them a toy-carriage, in which he placed a doll dressed as Puss-in-boots.

"It is the carriage of the Marquis of Carabas, my children," he said, as they went to the Permons' house by the river. "And when I am at Valence, you will look at this, and think again of your friend, Lieutenant Puss-in-Boots."

But between the date of his commission and his orders to join his regiment at Valence a whole month passed, in which time Napoleon's funds ran very low. Indeed, he was so completely penniless, that, when the orders did come, Napoleon had nothing; and his friend Alexander had just enough to get them both to Lyons.

"What shall we do? I have nothing left, Napoleon," said Alexander; "and Valence is still miles away."

"We can walk, Alexander," said Napoleon.

"But one must eat, my friend," Alexander replied ruefully. For boys of sixteen have good appetites, and do not like to go hungry.

"True, one must eat," said Napoleon. "Ah, I have it! We will call upon Monsieur Barlet." Now, Monsieur Barlet was a friend of the Bonapartes, and had once lived in Corsica. So both boys hunted him up, and Napoleon told their story.

"Well, my valiant soldiers of the king," laughed Monsieur Barlet, "what is the best way out? Come; fall back on your training at the military school. What line of conduct, my Napoleon, would you adopt, if you were besieged in a fortress and were destitute of provisions?"

"My faith, sir," answered Napoleon promptly, "so long as there were any provisions in the enemy's camp I would never go hungry."

Monsieur Barlet laughed heartily.

"By which you mean," he said, "that I am the enemy's camp, and you propose to forage on me for provisions, eh? Good, very good, that! See, then, I surrender. Accept, most noble warriors, a tribute from the enemy."

And with that he gave the boys a little money, and a letter of introduction to his friend at Valence, the Abbe (or Reverend) Saint Raff.

But Lyons is a pleasant city, where there is much to see and plenty to do. So, when the boys left Lyons, they had spent most of Monsieur Barlet's "tip"; and, to keep the balance for future use, they fell back on their original intention, and walked all the way from Lyons to Valence.

Thus it was that Napoleon joined his regiment; and on the fifth of November 1785, he and Alexander, foot-sore, but full of boyish spirits, entered the old garrison-town of Valence in Southern France, and were warmly welcomed by Alexander's older brother, Captain Gabriel des Mazes, of the La Fere regiment, who at once took the boys in charge, and introduced them to their new life as soldiers of the garrison of Valence.

CHAPTER SEVENTEEN.

DARK DAYS.

It does not take boys and girls long to find out that realization is not always equal to anticipation. Especially is this so with thoughtful, sober-minded boys like the young Napoleon.

At first, on his arrival at Valence, as lieutenant in his regiment, he set out to have a good time.

He took lodging with an old maid who let out rooms to young officers, in a house on Grand Street, in the town of Valence. Her name was Mademoiselle Bon. She kept a restaurant and billiard - room; and Napoleon's room was on the first floor, fronting the street, and next to the noisy billiard - room. This was not a particularly favorable place for a boy to pursue his studies; and at first Napoleon seem disposed to make the most of what boys would call his "freedom." He went to balls and parties; became a "great talker;" took dancing lessons of Professor Dautre, and tried to become what is called a "society man."

But it suited neither his tastes nor his desires, and made a large hole in his small pay as lieutenant. Indeed, after paying for his board and lodging, he had left only about seven dollars a month to spend for clothes and "fun." So he soon tired of this attempt to keep up appearances on a little money. He took to his books again, studying philosophy, geography, history, and mathematics. He thought he might make a living by his pen, and concluded to become an author. So he began writing a history of his native island - Corsica.

He even tried a novel, but boys of seventeen are not very well fitted for real literary work, and his first attempts were but poor affairs. His reading in history and geography drew his attention to Asia; and he always had a boyish dream of what he should like to attempt and achieve in the half-fabled land of India, where he believed great success and vast riches were to be secured by an ambitious young man, who had knowledge of military affairs, and the taste for leadership. At last he was ordered away on active service; first to suppress what was known as the "Two-cent Rebellion" in Lyons, and after that to the town of Douay in Belgium.

If was while there that bad news came to him from Corsica. His family was again in trouble. His mother had tried silkworm raising, and failed; his uncle the canon was very sick; his good friend and the patron of the family, General Marbeuf, was dead; his brothers were unsuccessful in getting positions or employment; and something must be done to help matters in the big bare house in Ajaccio.

Worried over the news, Napoleon tried to get leave of absence, so as to go to Corsica and see what he could do. But this favor was not granted him. His anxiety made him low-spirited; this brought on an attack of fever. The leave of absence was granted him because he was sick; and early in 1787 he went home to Corsica.

He had been absent from home for eight years. At once he tried to set matters on a better footing. He fixed up the little house at Melilli, which had belonged to his mother's father; tried to help his mother in her attempts at mulberry-growing for the silkworms; saw that his brother Joseph was enabled to go into the oil-trade; brightened up his uncle the canon with his political discussions and a correspondence with a famous French physician as to the cure for his uncle's gout; and finally, being recalled to his regiment, went back to Paris, and joined his regiment at Auxonne.

While in garrison at this place, he lodged with Professor Lombard, a teacher of mathematics, whom he sometimes assisted in his classes. He worked hard, kept out of debt, ate little, and was "poor, but proud." He gained the esteem of his superiors; for in a letter to Joey Fesch, who was now a priest, he wrote:

> "The general here thinks very well of me; so much so, that he has ordered me to construct a polygon, - works for which great calculations are necessary, - and I am hard at work at the head of two hundred men. This unheard-of mark of favor has somewhat irritated the captains against me; they declare it is insulting to them that a lieutenant should be intrusted with so important a work, and that, when more than thirty men are employed, one of them should not have been sent out also. My comrades also have shown some jealousy, but it will pass. What troubles me is my health, which does not seem to me very good."

Indeed, it was not very good. He was just at the age when a young fellow needs all the good food, healthful exercise, and restful sleep that are possible; and these Napoleon did not permit himself. The doctor of his regiment told him he must take better care of himself; but that he did not, we know from this scrap from a letter to his mother: -

"I have no resources but work. I dress but once in eight days, for the Sunday parade. I sleep but little since my illness; it is incredible. I go to bed at ten o'clock, and get up at four in the morning. I take but one meal a day, at three o'clock. But that is good for my health."

The boy probably added that last line to keep his mother from feeling anxious. But it was not true. Such a life for a growing boy is very bad for his health. Again Napoleon fell ill, obtained six months' sick leave, and went again to Corsica. This visit was a much longer one than the first. In fact, he overstayed his leave; got into trouble with the authorities because of this; smoothed it over; regained his health; wrote and worked; mixed himself up in Corsican politics; became a fiery young advocate of liberty; and at last, after a year's absence from France, returned to join his regiment at Auxonne, taking with him his young brother, Louis, whom he had agreed to support and educate.

It was quite a burden for this young man of twenty to assume. But Napoleon undertook it cheerfully, he was glad to be able to do anything that should lighten his mother's burdens.

The brothers did not have a particularly pleasant home at Auxonne. They lived in a bare room in the regimental barracks, "Number 16," up one flight of stairs. It was wretchedly furnished. It contained an uncurtained bed, a table, two chairs, and an old wooden box, which the boys used, both as bureau and bookcase. Louis slept on a little cot-bed near his brother; and how they lived on sixty cents a day - paying out of that for food, lodging, clothes, and books - is one of the mysteries.

In fact, they nearly starved themselves. Napoleon made the broth; brushed and mended their clothes; sometimes had only dry bread for a meal; and, as Napoleon said later, "bolted the door on his poverty." That is to say, they went nowhere, and saw no one.

It was hard on the young lieutenant; it was perhaps even harder on the little brother.

One morning, after Napoleon had dressed himself and was preparing their poor breakfast, he knocked on the floor with his cane to arouse his brother and call him to breakfast and studies.

Little Louis awoke so slowly that Napoleon was obliged to arouse him a second time.

"Come, come, my Louis," he cried; "what is the matter this morning? It seems to me that you are very lazy."

"Oh, brother!" answered the half-awaked child, "I was having such a beautiful dream!"

"And what did you dream?" asked Napoleon.

The little Louis sat upright on the edge of his cot. "I dreamed that I was a king," he replied.

"A king! Well, well!" exclaimed his brother, laughing. Then he glanced around at the bare and poverty-stricken room. "And what, then, your Majesty, was I, your brother, - an emperor perhaps?" Then he shrugged his shoulders, and pinched his brother's ear.

"Well, kings and emperors must eat and work," he said, "the same as lieutenants and schoolboys. Come, then, King Louis; some broth, and then to your duty."

This was Napoleon at twenty, - a poverty-pinched, self-sacrificing, hard-working boy, a man before his time; knowing very little of fun and comfort, and very much of toil and trouble.

He was an ill-proportioned young man, not yet having outgrown the "spindling" appearance of his boyhood, but even then he possessed certain of the remarkable features familiar to every boy and girl who has studied the portraits of Napoleon the emperor. His head was large and finely shaped, with a wide forehead, large mouth, and straight nose, a projecting chin, and large, steel-blue eyes, that were full of fire and power. His face was sallow, his hair brown and stringy, his cheeks lean from not too much over-feeding. His body and lees were thin and small, but his chest was broad, and his neck short and thick. His step was firm and steady, with nothing of the "wobbly" gait we often see in people who are not well-proportioned. His character was undoubtedly that of a young man who had the desire to get ahead faster than his opportunities would permit. Solitude had made him uncommunicative and secretive; anxiety and privation had made him self-helpful and self-reliant; lack of sympathy had made him calculating; but doing for others had made him kind-hearted and generous. His reading and study had made him ambitious; his knowledge that when he knew a thing he really knew it, made him masterful and desirous of leadership. He had few of the vices, and sowed but a small crop of what is called the "wild oats" of youth; he abhorred debt, and scarcely ever owed a penny, even when in sorest straits; and, while not a bright nor a great scholar, what he had learned he was able to store away in his brain, to be drawn upon for use when, in later years, this knowledge could be used to advantage.

Such at twenty years of age was Napoleon Bonaparte. Such he remained through the years of his young manhood, meeting all sorts of discouragements, facing the hardest poverty, becoming disgusted with many things that occurred in those changing days, when liberty was replacing tyranny, and the lesson of free America was being read and committed by the world.

He saw the turmoil and terrors of the French Revolution - that season of blood, when a long-suffering people struck a blow at tyranny, murdered their king, and tried to build on the ruins of an overturned kingdom an impossible republic.

You will understand all this better when you come to read the history of France, and see through how many noble but mistaken efforts that fair European land struggled from tyranny to freedom. In these efforts Napoleon had a share; and it was his boyhood of privation and his youth of discouragement that made him a man of purpose, of persistence and endeavor, raising him step by step, in the days when men needed leaders but found none, until this one finally proved himself a leader indeed, and, grasping the reins of command, advanced steadily from the barracks to a throne. All this is history; it is the story of the development and progress of the most remarkable man of modern times. You can read the story in countless books; for now, after Napoleon has been dead for over seventy years, the world is learning to sift the truth from all the chaff of falsehood and fable that so long surrounded him; it is endeavoring to place this marvellous leader of men in the place he should rightly occupy - that of a great man, led by ambition and swayed by selfishness, but moved also by a desire to do noble things for the nation that he had raised to greatness, and the men who looked to him for guidance and direction.

Our story of his boyhood ends here. For years after he came to young manhood fate seemed against him, and privation held him down. But he broke loose from all entanglements; he surmounted all obstacles; he conquered all adverse circumstances. He rose to power by his own abilities. He led the armies of France to marvellous victories. He became the idol of his soldiers, the hero of the people, the chief man in the nation, the controlling power in Europe; and on the second of December, in the year 1804, he was crowned in the great church of Notre Dame, in Paris, Emperor of the French. "Straw-nose," the poverty-stricken little Corsican, had become the foremost man in all the world!

But through all his marvellous career he never forgot his family. The same love and devotion that he bestowed upon them when a poor boy and a struggling lieutenant, he lavished upon them as general, consul, and emperor. Indeed, to them was due, to a certain extent, his later misfortunes, and his fall from power. The more generous he became, the more selfish did his brothers and sisters grow. For their interests he neglected his own safety and the welfare of France. His unselfishness was, indeed, his greatest selfishness; and the boy who uncomplainingly took his sister's punishment for the theft of the basket of fruit, stood also as the scapegoat for all the mistakes and stupidities and wrong-doings that were due to his self-seeking brothers and sisters, the Bonaparte children of Ajaccio in Corsica.

CHAPTER EIGHTEEN.

BY THE WALL OF THE SOLDIERS' HOME.

The Emperor Napoleon had long been dead. A wasting disease and English indignities had worn his life away upon his prison-rock of St. Helena; and, after many years, his body had been brought back to France, and placed beneath a mighty monument in the splendid Home for Invalid Soldiers, in the beautiful city of Paris which he had loved so much, and where his days of greatness and power had been spent.

There, beneath the dome, surrounded by all the life and brilliancy of the great city, he rests. His last wish has been gratified - the wish he expressed in the will he wrote on his prison-rock, so many miles away: "I desire that my ashes shall rest by the banks of the Seine, in the midst of the French people I have loved so well."

That Home for Invalid Soldiers, in which now stands the tomb of Napoleon, has long been, as its name implies, a home for the maimed and aged veterans who have fought in the armies of France, and received as their portion, wounds, illness, - and glory.

The sun shines brightly upon the walls of the great home; and the war-worn veterans dearly love to bask in its life-giving rays, or to rest in the shade of its towering walls.

It was on a certain morning, many years ago, that I who write these lines - Eugenie Foa, friend to all the boys and girls who love to read of glorious and heroic deeds - was resting upon one of the seats near to the shade-giving walls of the Soldiers' Home. As I sat there, several of the old soldiers placed themselves on the adjoining seat. There were a half-dozen of them - all veterans, grizzled and gray, and ranging from the young veteran of fifty to the patriarch of ninety years.

As is always the case with these scarred old fellows, their talk speedily turned upon the feats at arms at which they had assisted. And this dialogue was so enlivening, so picturesque, so full of the hero-spirit that lingers ever about the walls of that noble building which is a hero's resting-place, that I gladly listened to their talk, and try now to repeat it to you.

"But those Egyptians whom Father Nonesuch, here, helped to conquer," one old fellow said, - "ah, they were great story-tellers! I have read of some of them in a mightily fine book. It was called the 'Tales of the Thousand and One Nights.'"

"Bah!" cried the eldest of the group. "Bah! I say. Your 'Thousand and One Nights,' your fairy stories, all the wonders of nature," - here he waved his trembling old hand excitedly, - "all these are but as nothing compared with what I have seen."

"Hear him!" exclaimed the young fellow of fifty; "hear old Father Nonesuch, will you, comrades? He thinks, because he has seen the republic, the consulate, the empire, the hundred days, the kingdom" -

"And is not that enough, youngster?" interrupted the old veteran they called Father Nonesuch.[1]

[1] Perhaps the correct rendering of this nickname would be "The Remnant," and it applies to the battered veteran even better than "Nonesuch."]

He certainly merited the nickname given him by his comrades; for I saw, by glancing at him, that the old veteran had but one leg, one arm, and one eye.

"Enough?" echoed the one called "the youngster," whose grizzled locks showed him to be at least fifty years old, "Enough? Well, perhaps - for you. But, my faith! I cannot see that they were finer than the 'Thousand and one Nights.'"

"Bah!" again cried old Nonesuch contemptuously; "but those were fairy stories, I tell you, youngster, - untrue stories, - pagan stories. But when one can tell, as can I, of stories that are true, - of history - history this - history that - true histories every one - bah!" and, shrugging his shoulders, old Nonesuch tapped upon his neighbor's snuff-box, and, with his only hand, drew out a mighty pinch by way of emphasis.

"Well, what say thou, Nonesuch, - you and your histories?" persisted the young admirer of the "Arabian Nights."

"As for me, - my faith! I like only marvellous."

he rests" - The Hotel des Invalides (The 'Soldiers' Home' in Paris, containing the Tomb of Napoleon)]

"And I tell you this, youngster," the old veteran cried, while his voice cracked into a tremble in his excitement, "there is more of the marvellous in the one little finger of my history than in all the characters you can crowd together in your 'Thousand and One Nights.' Bah! - Stephen, boy; light my pipe."

"And what is your history, Father Nonesuch?" demanded "the youngster," while two-armed Stephen, a gray old "boy" of seventy, filled and lighted the old veteran's pipe.

"My history?" cried old Nonesuch, struggling to his feet, - or rather to his foot, - and removing his hat, "it is, my son, that of the Emperor Napoleon!"

And at the word, each old soldier sprang also to his feet, and removed his hat silently and in reverence.

"Why, youngster!" old Father Nonesuch continued, dropping again to the bench, "if one wished to relate about my emperor a thousand and one stories a thousand and one nights; to see even a thousand and one days increased by a thousand and one battles, adding to that a thousand and one victories, one would have a thousand and a million million things - fine, glorious, delightful, to hear. For, remember, comrades," and the old man well-nigh exploded with his mathematical calculation, and the grandeur of his own recollections, "remember you this: I never left the great Napoleon!"

"Ah, yes," another aged veteran chimed in; "ah, yes; he was a great man."

Old Nonesuch clapped his hand to his ear.

"Pardon me, comrade the Corsican," he said, with the air of one who had not heard aright; "excuse my question, but would you kindly tell me whom you call a great man?"

"Whom, old deaf ears? Why, the Emperor Napoleon, of course," replied the Corsican.

Old Nonesuch burst out laughing, and pounded the pavement with his heavy cane.

"To call the emperor a man!" he exclaimed; "and what, then, will you call me?"

"You? why, what should we?" said the Corsican veteran; "old Father Nonesuch, old 'Not Entire,' otherwise, Corporal Francis Haut of Brienne."

"Ah, bah!" cried the persistent veteran; "I do not mean my name, stupid! I mean my quality, my - my title, my - well - my sex, - indeed, what am I?" "Well, what is left of you, I suppose," laughed the Corsican, "we might call a man."

"A man! there you have it exactly!" cried old Nonesuch. "I am a man; and so are you, Corsican, and you, Stephen, and you, - almost so, - youngster. But my emperor - the Emperor Napoleon! was he a man? Away with you! It was the English who invented that story; they did not know what he was capable of, those English! The emperor a man? Bah!"

"What was he, then? A woman?" queried the Corsican.

"Ah, stupid one! where are your wits?" cried old Nonesuch, shaking pipe and cane excitedly. "Are you, then, as dull as those English? Why, the emperor was - the emperor! It is we, his soldiers, who were men."

The Corsican veteran shook his head musingly.

"It may be so; it may be so, good Nonesuch. I do not say no to you," he said. "Ah, my dear emperor! I have seen him often. I knew him when he was small; I knew him when he was grown. I saw him born; I saw him die" - "Halt there!" cried old Nonesuch; "let me stop you once more, good comrade Corsican. Do not make these other 'Not Entires' swallow such impossible and indigestible things. The emperor was never born; the emperor never died; the emperor has always been; the emperor always will be. To prove it," he added quickly, holding up his cane, as he saw that the Corsican was about to protest at this surprising statement, "to prove it, let me tell you. He fought at Constantine; he fought at St. Jean d'Ulloa; he fought at Sebastopol, and was conqueror."

"Come, come, Father Nonesuch!" broke in "the youngster," and others of that group of veterans, "you are surely wandering. It was not the Emperor Napoleon who fought at those places. That was long after he was dead. It was the son of Louis Philippe, the Duke of Nemours, who fought at Constantine; it was the Prince of Joinville who led at Ulloa; and, at Sebastopol, the" -

"Bah!" broke in the old veteran. "You are all owls, you! What if they did? I will not deny either the Duke of Nemours nor the Prince of Joinville, nor Louis Philippe himself. But what then? You need not deny, you youngster, nor you, the other shouters, that when the cannons boom, when the battles rage, when, above all, one is conqueror for France, there is something of my emperor in that. Could they have conquered except for him? Ten thousand bullets! I say. He is everywhere."

"But, see here, Father Nonesuch," protested the Corsican, "you must not deny to me the emperor's birth; for I know, I know all about it. Was not my mother, Saveria, Madame Letitia's servant? Was she not, too, nurse to the little Napoleon? She was, my faith! And she has told me a hundred times all about him. I know of what I speak. Our emperor, Napoleon Bonaparte, was born on the fifteenth of August, 1769, and when he was a baby, the cradle not being at hand, he was laid upon a rug in Madame Letitia's room. And on that rug was a fine representation of Mars, the god of war. And because his bed on that rug was on the very spot which represented Mars, that, old Nonesuch, is why our emperor was ever valiant in war. What say you to that?"

"Oh, very well, very well," said old Nonesuch, as if he made a great concession; "if you say so from your own knowledge, if you insist that he was born, let it go so. I admit that he was born. But as to his being dead, eh? Will you insist on that too?"

"And why not?" replied the Corsican, still harping on his personal knowledge of things in Ajaccio. "I knew the Bonapartes well, I tell you. There was the father, Papa Charles, a fine, noble-looking man; and their uncle, the canon - ah! he was a good man. He was short and fat and bald, with little eyes, but with a look like an eagle. And the children! how often I have seen them, though they were older than I - Joseph and Lucien, and little Louis, and Eliza and Pauline and Caroline. Yes; I saw them often. And Napoleon too.

They say he never played much. But you knew him at Brienne school, old Nonesuch."

"Yes," nodded the old veteran; "for there my father was the porter."

"He was ever grave and stern, was Napoleon; - not wicked, though" - "No, no; never wicked," broke in old Nonesuch. "I remember his snow-ball fight."

"A fight with snow-balls!" exclaimed the youngster. "Yes; with snow-balls, youngster," replied old Nonesuch.

"Did you never hear of it? But you are too young. Only the Corsican and I can remember that;" and the old man nodded to the Corsican with the superiority of old age over these "babies," as he called the younger veterans. "Let me see," said Nonesuch, crossing his wooden leg over his leg of flesh; "I was the porter's boy at Brienne school. I was there to blacken my shoes - not mine, you understand, but those of the scholars. There was much snow that winter. The scholars could not play in the courts nor out-of-doors. They were forced to walk in the halls. That wearied them, but it rejoiced me. Why? Because I had but few shoes to blacken. They could not get them dirty while they remained indoors. But, look you! one day at recess I saw the scholars all out-of-doors, - all out in the snow. 'Alas! alas! my poor shoes,' said I. It made me sad. I hid behind the greenhouse doors, to see the meaning of this disorder. Then I heard a sudden shout. 'Brooms, brooms! shovels, shovels!' they cried. They rushed into the greenhouse: they took whatever they could find; and one boy, who saw me standing idle, pushed me toward the door, crying, 'Here, lazy-bones! take a shovel, take a broom! Get to work, and help us!' - 'Help you do what?' said I. 'To make the fort and roll snow-balls,' he replied. 'Not I; it is too cold,' I answered. Then the boys laughed at me. My faith! to-day I think they were right. Then they tried to push me out-of-doors, I resisted; I would not go. Suddenly appeared one whom I did not know. He said nothing. He simply looked at me. He signed to me to take a broom - to march into the garden - to set to work. And I obeyed. I dared not resist. I did whatever he told me; and, my faith! so, too, did all the boys. 'Is this one a teacher?' I asked one of the scholars. 'He does not look so; he is too small and pale and thin.' - 'No,' replied the boy; 'it is Napoleon.' - 'And who is Napoleon?' I asked; for at that time I was as ignorant as all of you here. 'Is he our patron? Is he the king? Is he the pope?' - 'No; he is Napoleon,' the boy replied again, shrugging his shoulders. I did not ask more. The boy was right. Napoleon was neither boy nor man, patron, king, nor pope; he was Napoleon! You should have seen him while we were working. His hand was pointing continually, - here, there, everywhere, - indicating what he wished to have done; his clear voice was ever explaining or commanding. Then, when we had cut paths in the snow, and had built ramparts, dug trenches, raised fortifications, rolled snow-balls - then the attack began. I had nothing more to do, I looked on. But my heart beat fast; I wished that I might fight also. But I was the porter's son, and did not dare to join in the scholars' play. Every day for a week, while the snow lasted, the war was fought at each recess. Snow-balls flew through the air, striking heads, faces, breasts, backs. The shouting and the tumult gave me great pleasure; but, oh! The shoes I had to blacken! Then I said to myself, 'I wish to be a soldier.' And I kept my word."

CHAPTER NINETEEN.

THE LITTLE CORPORAL.

"But why," asked the Corsican, as old Nonesuch concluded his story, and all the veterans applauded with cane and boot, "why did you not say, 'I wish to be a general,' and keep your word. Others like you have been soldiers of the emperor - and generals, marshals, princes."

"Yes, Corsican," replied old Nonesuch sadly; "what you say is true. But I will tell you what prevented my advancement. I did not know how to read as well as a lot of the schemers who were in my regiment. In fact," old Nonesuch confessed, "I could not write; I could not read at all."

"Why did you not learn, then, father?" asked one of the veterans, who, because he sat up late every night to read the daily paper, was called by his comrades "the scholar."

"I did try to learn, Mr. Scholar," replied old Nonesuch, taking a pinch of snuff from the Corsican's box; "but indeed it was not in the blood, don't you see? Not one of my family could read or write; and then I saw so much trouble over the pens and the books when I was blackening my boots at Brienne school, that then I had no wish to learn. 'It is all vexation,' I said. And when I became a soldier, what do you suppose prevented my learning?"

"Were your brains shot away, old Nonesuch?" queried the scholar sarcastically.

"My brains, say you!" the old man cried indignantly. "And if they had been, Mr. Scholar, I would still have more than you. No; it was an adventure I had after Austerlitz. Ah, what a battle was that! I had the good luck there to have this leg that I have not now, carried away by a cannon-ball" -

"Good luck! says he," broke in the youngster. "And how good luck, Father Nonesuch?"

"Tut, tut! boys are so impatient," said old Nonesuch with a frown. "Yes, youngster, good luck, said I. Well, one day, after I had my timber-toe put on, the emperor, who always had thoughts for those of his soldiers who had been wounded, gave notice that he had certain small places at his disposal which he wished to distribute among us crippled ones, in order that we might rest from war. Then all of us set to wondering, 'What can I do? What shall I ask for? What do I like best to do?' My wish was never to leave my own general. He was General Junot" -

"Ah, yes! I know of him," said the Corsican. "He married a Corsican girl, Laura Permon, a friend of the Bonaparte children."

"The same," old Nonesuch said, with a nod at his comrade. "Now, I saw that the person who was nearest to my General Junot was his secretary. One day, when

I was at Paris, the emperor, I was told, was to review his troops in the courtyard of the Tuileries; so I dressed myself in my best, - it was a grenadier's uniform, - a comrade wrote on a piece of paper my desire; and, with my paper in my hand, I posted myself near a battalion of lancers. 'The emperor will see me here,' said I. In truth, he did come; he did see me. He came towards me, and, with the look that pierced me through, - ten thousand bullets! as the plough cuts through the ground, - 'Are you not an Egyptian, my grenadier?' he asked me. (You know, Corsican, he called all of us Egyptians who had fought with him in Egypt.) 'Yes, my Emperor,' I replied, so glorified to see that he recognized me, that, my faith! my heart swelled and swelled, so that I thought it would crack with pride, and burst my coat open. The emperor took the paper I held out toward him. He read it. 'So, so, my Egyptian! you wish to be a secretary, eh?' - 'Yes, my Emperor,' I answered. 'Do you know how to read and write?' said he. 'Eh? Why! I know not if I know,' said I. 'What! You do not know if you know?' he repeated. 'Why, no, my Emperor,' said I; 'for, look you! I have never tried; but perhaps I do know.' The emperor pulled my ear, as much as to say, 'Well, here is an odd one!' 'But,' said he, 'to be a secretary one must know how to read and write, comrade.' He called me his comrade, see you - me, who had blackened his shoes at Brienne. I was the emperor's comrade. He had said it. The tears came to my eyes for joy. 'Ah, then, my Emperor, let us say no more about it,' said I. 'But if you would promise to learn,' said he. 'Oh, as for that, my Emperor,' I answered, 'by the faith of an Egyptian of the guard, second division, first battalion! I do not promise it to you.' - 'Then ask me something else,' said he. I hesitated. I did not know how to say just what I wished to ask; for it was worth to me very much more than the place of secretary. 'Come, then, comrade; speak quickly,' said the emperor; 'what is it you wish?' - 'I wish, my Emperor,' I stammered, 'to press my lips to your hand.'"

"Ho! was that all?" cried the youngster.

"All!" echoed the Nonesuch, turning upon the youngest veteran a look of scorn. "All! It was more than anything!"

"Well, and what said the emperor?" asked Stephen breathlessly.

"He said nothing," responded Nonesuch. "He smiled; then instantly I felt his hand in mine. I wonder I did not die with joy. I kissed his hand. He grasped mine firmly. 'Thanks, my comrade,' he said. 'My Emperor,' I said, 'I promise you never to learn to read and write.' And I said no more. And that, comrades, is why I never learned."

"Which hand was it?" asked the youngster with interest.

"This one, thank God!" cried the veteran. "The other I lost at Jena. No, I never learned to write; the hand that the emperor had clasped in his should never, I vowed, be dishonored by a pen. I look at this hand with veneration. See! it has been pressed by my emperor. I love it; I honor it. Indeed, at one time I thought of cutting it off, - that was before Jena, - and putting it in a frame, that I might have it always before my eyes. But my General Junot, to whom I told my plan, said that then it would be spoiled forever, and that the only way not to lose sight of it was to let it always hang to my arm; thus, he said, it would always be beside me. That is how you see it still, comrades. To write, to write - bah! It always troubles me," old Nonesuch continued musingly, as he regarded his precious hand, "when I see those poor fellows, their noses over a bit of paper, their bodies bent double! Writing is not a man's proper state; it does not agree with his valiant and warlike nature. Talk to me of a charge, of an onset! that is the true vocation; that is why the good God created the human race. One - two - three - shoulder arms! that is clear; that is easily understood. But to study a dozen letters; to remember which is *b* and which is *o,* and that *b* and *o* make *bo*! that is not meant for the head. I prefer to read a battle with my musket and my sword. Pif! paf! pouf! that is the way I read. And now that I can read no more, I have but one pleasure, - to tell of my battles. Is not that better than your 'Thousand and One Nights,' youngster?"

"You have, indeed, much to tell, old Nonesuch," replied the youngster guardedly, "and you have, indeed, seen much."

"Ah, have I not, though!" old Nonesuch responded. "Do you not remember, Corsican, in the third year of the republic, as our government was then called, how the word came: 'The English are in Toulon! Soldiers of France, you must dislodge them!'?"

"Ah, do I not, old Nonesuch! I was a conscript then," replied the Corsican.

"So, too, was I," said the old veteran. "We marched to Toulon. The next day there was an action. I ate a kind of small pills I had never tasted at Paris. The English and the French kept up a conversation with these sugar-plums. Our dialogue went on for days. They would toss their sugar-plums into the town; we would throw these plums back to them, especially into one bonbon box. You remember that box - that fort, Corsican, do you not?"

"What, the Little Gibraltar?" queried the Corsican.

"The same," replied old Nonesuch, "for so the English called it. But they had to give it up. We filled the Little Gibraltar so full of our sugar-plums that the English had to get out. Then it was that I saw a thin little captain at the guns. I knew him at once. It was Bonaparte of Brienne school. This is what he did. An artillery man was killed while charging his piece. I do not know how many had been cut off at that same gun. It was warm - it was hot there, I can tell you! No one wished to approach it. Then my little captain - my Bonaparte of Brienne - dashed at the gun. He loaded it; he was not killed. Oh, what a pleasure-party that was! There he met two other tough ones like himself, - Duroc and Junot. Ah, that Junot! He became my general later. He was a cool joker. Napoleon wished some one to write for him. He asked for a corporal or a sergeant who could write and stand fire at the same time. Sergeant Junot came to him. 'Write!' said Napoleon. And as Junot wrote, look you a cannon-ball ploughed the earth at his feet, and scattered the dirt over his paper. 'Good!' cried this Junot, never looking up from his paper. 'I needed sand to blot my ink.' That made Napoleon his friend forever. Then those in power at Paris took offence at something Napoleon did. They called him back to Paris. He was disgraced. But he had courage, had my Napoleon. He cared nothing for those stupid ones at Paris. 'I will make them see,' said he, 'that I am master.' He took post for Paris.

Everything was wrong there. Every one was hungry. They fought for bread, as horses when there is no hay in the rack. Then, crack! Napoleon came. In two moves he had established order. Then who so great as he? He was made general. He was sent to Italy. He fought at Lodi. You remember Lodi, Corsican?"

"Ha! the fight on the bridge; do I not, though!" the Corsican answered excitedly. "It was there he led everything; it was there he conquered everything; it was there he sighted the cannon against the Austrians; it was there he led us straight across the bridge; it was there we cheered for him, and called him the 'Little Corporal!'"

"Eh, was it not! Cheer for the Little Corporal, comrades!" cried old Nonesuch, swinging his hat; and all the veterans sprang up, and stamped and shouted: "Long live the Little Corporal!"

"As he has!" said old Nonesuch. "See you, Corsican! what said I? The emperor lives, I tell you!"

"And that was Italy, was it?" said the scholar.

"Yes; that was Italy," the veteran replied. "It was there we were going; and, with our Little Corporal to lead us, turned everything into victory."

"Tell us of it, Father Nonesuch," demanded the youngster.

"Yes; tell us of it," echoed the younger veterans, their scarred old faces full of interest and excitement. "I will, my children. It was thus, you see," - puff - puff, "eh - Stephen, fill my pipe again!"

So Stephen filled the old fellow's pipe again, and set it aglow; and all the others waited, silently watchful, until, after a few puffs and whiffs, the old veteran began again.

CHAPTER TWENTY.

"LONG LIVE THE EMPEROR!"

"It was thus, you see," said old Nonesuch, crossing his legs - the wooden one over the good one. "At that time our army in Italy was destitute of everything. We had nothing - no bread, no ammunition, no shoes, no coats. Ah, it was a poor army we were then! The people at Paris, called the Directory, were worried over our condition. The army must have bread, ammunition, shoes, coats, they said. We must send one to look after this. And, as I told you, they sent Napoleon. It was in March, in the year 1796, that he came to us at Nice. We were near by, in camp at Abbenya. There the new general held his first review. He looked at us; he pitied us. 'Soldiers!' he said to us, 'you are naked; you are badly fed. The government owes you much; it can give you nothing. You are in need of everything, - boots, bread, soup! Well, I will lead you into the most fertile plains in the world. I have come to take you into a country where you will find everything in plenty, - dollars, cattle, roast-meat, salads, honor, palaces, what you will. Soldiers of Italy, how do you like that?'"

"Ah! but that was grand," cried the youngster; "and you said?"

"We said, 'How do we like it, my general? Ten

thousand bullets! March you at our head, and you will see how we like it.' His words gave us new heart; his promises seemed already to clothe us. We were ragged and tired; but it seemed, after that speech, as if we walked on air, and were dressed in silken robes. Forward, march! Boom - boom - boom! Ta-ra, ta-ra-ra! Hear the drums! See us marching! We marched through the day; we marched through the night. We were faint with hunger, but we marched. We were at Montenotte on the eleventh of April. We whacked the Austrians, - famous men, nevertheless; well furnished, good fighters! But, bah! what was that to us? We whacked them at Montenotte. They ran; we after them. We fell upon then at Millesimo, at Dego, at Mondovi, at Cherasco. We had a taste of the glory of being conquerors. We routed the Austrians in those fights that were called 'the Five Days' Campaign.' We had brave generals with us; and we had Napoleon! From the heights of Ceva he showed us the plains of Italy, - the rich, well-watered land which he had promised us. Then we crossed the Alps. Mighty mountains! Bah! what of that? We were Frenchmen; we had Napoleon! We turned the flank of the Alps. We fought at Fombio; we fought on the bridge of Lodi; we marched into Milan. We were Frenchmen; we had Napoleon! In fact, we conquered Italy! We fought at Arcola; we conquered at Rivoli. Then who so great as the Little Corporal? We planted the eagles upon the lion of Saint Mark, at Venice - a famous lion, nevertheless. But who could resist us? We had Napoleon! Then we returned to Toulon. Then Napoleon said, 'Soldiers! two years ago you had nothing. I made promises to you; have I kept them?' - 'You have; you have, my general!' every man of us shouted. 'Will you follow me again?' said Napoleon. 'To the death, my general!' we shouted once more. Behold us now embarked in ships. 'And now, what place are we to conquer?' we asked our generals. 'Egypt,' they answered. 'It is well,' we said. 'We will go to Egypt; we will take Egypt.'

"My faith! but you were brave, you old soldiers," cried the youngster with enthusiasm. "But think of it, then! To Egypt!"

"Well, we took Egypt," resumed old Nonesuch. "We were Frenchmen. We had Napoleon! And after that we undertook another little campaign in Italy. Then we returned to France, our beautiful France, to install ourselves in the Tuileries. Eh!" - puff - puff, - "Light my pipe, Stephen!"

And Stephen again lighted the old veteran's pipe.

"Yes; in the Tuileries" - puff - puff. "We gave ourselves up to *fetes*. Ah! there were grand times - each one finer than the other. One might call them *fetes* indeed! Death of my life! Who was it said just now that the emperor was a man? Why, look you! his enemies - those villains of traitors - tried to kill him. They plotted against him. But, bah! They could not. He rode over infernal machines as if they were roses. They could not kill him. Those things are for men - for little kings. He was Napoleon!"

"And at last he was crowned emperor," suggested the youngster.

"Yes; on the second of December, in the year 1804," answered old Nonesuch. "And the Pope himself came from Rome to consecrate our emperor. Ah, then, what *fetes*, my comrades! what *fetes* and *fetes* and *fetes*! It rained kings on all sides."

"But there came an end of *fetes*" said the scholar, who read in books and newspapers.

"Well, what would you have? - always feasting? Perhaps you think that our emperor once an emperor, would rest at home. Yes? Well, that would have been good for you and me; but he had still to undertake battles and victories, - battles and victories; they were the same thing! We were at Austerlitz; there I left this leg. At Jena; there I dropped this hand. Then came the peace, made upon the raft at Tilsit; then the war in Spain - a villanous war, and one I did not like at all. Napoleon was not there. Where he was not, the sun did not shine. Then we returned to Paris. The emperor married a grand princess. He had a son - a baby son - the King of Rome! Then, too, what *fetes!* A fine child the King of Rome! I saw him often in his little goat-carriage at the Tuileries. I do not know what has become of him. They say he is dead; but I do not believe that, any more than I believe that my emperor is dead. Two deaths? Bah! old women's stories, - witch stories, good only to frighten children to sleep. When my emperor and his son come back, we shall be amazed that we ever believed them dead!"

"But he disappeared - the emperor disappeared - he vanished," persisted the scholar.

"Yes; he disappeared," the veteran admitted. "For after that came the Russian Campaign. Ah, but it was a cold one! Such snow, such ice; so cold, so cold! It was then I lost my eye. My leg I left at Austerlitz, my arm at Jena; my eye I dropped somewhere in the Beresina, - so much the better. I could not see that freeze-out. Then they sent me here. And since that I do not know what has happened. They tell me - you tell me - much.

But to believe such foolish stories! Bah! I am not a baby. They tell me that the emperor - my emperor - was exiled to Elba; that he returned again to France; that he reigned a hundred days; that a battle was fought at - where was it?"

"Waterloo," suggested the scholar.

"Eh, yes, you say, at Waterloo; and you say we lost it? As if we could lose a battle, and Napoleon there! Then you will say that the empire was no longer an empire, but a kingdom; and that he who governed was called Louis the Eighteenth, and others after him, but not my emperor. Bah! foolish stories all!"

"But they are true, old Nonesuch," said the youngster sadly.

"Yes; they are true," echoed the other veterans. And the scholar added, "Yes; and your emperor was banished by those rascal English to a rock - the rock of St. Helena - a horrid rock, miles and miles out in the ocean. But he is here among us again." The Soldiers' Home, in the midst of his veterans, in the heart of his beautiful Paris.

Old soldiers are apt to be boastful when they tell, as did the Nonesuch, of the deeds of a leader whom they so often followed to victory. Madame Foa's pen has long since stopped its task of writing of French heroism for the boys and girls of France; but it never wrote anything more attractive or inspiring than the delicious bit of boasting that it put into the mouth of this dear and battered old veteran of Napoleon's wars, - Corporal Nonesuch of the Soldiers' Home.

For, if the American boys and girls who have followed this story will read, as I trust they will, the entire life-story of this marvelous man, - Napoleon Bonaparte, Emperor of the French, - they will learn that much of the boasting of old Nonesuch was true story, as he assured his comrades; while some of it, too, was, - let us say, the exaggeration of enthusiasm.

But there was much in the career of the great Napoleon to inspire enthusiasm. The determined and persistent way in which, while but a boy, he climbed steadily up, using the obstacles in his path but as the rounds of a ladder to lift him higher, affords a lesson of pluck and energy that every boy and girl can take to heart; while the story of his later career, through the rapid changes that made him general, consul, conqueror, emperor, is as full of interest, marvel, and romance as any of those wonder-stories of the "Arabian Nights" for which "the youngster" expressed so much admiration, but which old Nonesuch so contemptuously cast aside.

There were dark sides to his character; there were shadows on his career, there were blots on his name. Ambition, selfishness, and the love of success, were alike his inspiration and his ruin. But, with these, he possessed also the qualities that led men to follow him enthusiastically and love him devotedly.

But people do not all see things alike in this world; and since the downfall and death of Napoleon, those who recall his name have either enshrined him as a hero or vilified him as a monster. Whichever side in this controversy you make take as, when you grow older, you read and ponder over the story of Napoleon, you will, I am sure, be ready to admit his greatness as an historic character his ability as a soldier, his energy as a ruler, and his eminence as a man. And in these you will see but the logical outgrowth of his self-reliance, his determination, and his pluck as a boy, when on the rocky shore of Corsica, or in the schools of France, he was turned aside by no obstacle, and conquered neither by privation nor persecution, but pressed steadily forward to his great and matchless career as leader, soldier, and ruler - the most commanding figure of the nineteenth century. I did not like at all. Napoleon was not there. Where he was not, the sun did not shine. Then we returned to Paris. The emperor married a grand princess. He had a son - a baby son - the King of Rome! Then, too, what *fetes*! A fine child the King of Rome! I saw him often in his little goat-carriage at the Tuileries. I do not know what has become of him. They say he is dead; but I do not believe that, any more than I believe that my emperor is dead. Two deaths? Bah! old women's stories, - witch stories, good only to frighten children to sleep. When my emperor and his son come back, we shall be amazed that we ever believed them dead!"

"But he disappeared - the emperor disappeared - he vanished," persisted the scholar.

"Yes; he disappeared," the veteran admitted. "For after that came the Russian Campaign. Ah, but it was a cold one! Such snow, such ice; so cold, so cold! It was then I lost my eye. My leg I left at Austerlitz, my arm at Jena; my eye I dropped somewhere in the Beresina, - so much the better. I could not see that freeze-out.

Choose from Thousands of 1stWorldLibrary Classics By

Adolphus William Ward	Clemence Housman	Gabrielle E. Jackson
Aesop	Confucius	Garrett P. Serviss
Agatha Christie	Cornelis DeWitt Wilcox	Gaston Leroux
Alexander Aaronsohn	Cyril Burleigh	George Ade
Alexander Kielland	D. H. Lawrence	Geroge Bernard Shaw
Alexandre Dumas	Daniel Defoe	George Ebers
Alfred Gatty	David Garnett	George Eliot
Alfred Ollivant	Don Carlos Janes	George MacDonald
Alice Duer Miller	Donald Keyhole	George Orwell
Alice Turner Curtis	Dorothy Kilner	George Tucker
Alice Dunbar	Dougan Clark	George W. Cable
Ambrose Bierce	E. Nesbit	George Wharton James
Amelia E. Barr	E.P.Roe	Gertrude Atherton
Andrew Lang	E. Phillips Oppenheim	Grace E. King
Andrew McFarland Davis	Edgar Allan Poe	Grant Allen
Anna Sewell	Edgar Rice Burroughs	Guillermo A. Sherwell
Annie Besant	Edith Wharton	Gulielma Zollinger
Annie Hamilton Donnell	Edward J. O'Biren	Gustav Flaubert
Annie Payson Call	John Cournos	H. A. Cody
Anton Chekhov	Edwin L. Arnold	H. B. Irving
Arnold Bennett	Eleanor Atkins	H. G. Wells
Arthur Conan Doyle	Elizabeth Cleghorn	H. H. Munro
Arthur Ransome	Gaskell	H. Irving Hancock
Atticus	Elizabeth Von Arnim	H. Rider Haggard
B. M. Bower	Ellem Key	H. W. C. Davis
Basil King	Emily Dickinson	Hamilton Wright Mabie
Bayard Taylor	Erasmus W. Jones	Hans Christian Andersen
Ben Macomber	Ernie Howard Pie	Harold Avery
Booth Tarkington	Ethel Turner	Harold McGrath
Bram Stoker	Ethel Watts Mumford	Harriet Beecher Stowe
C. Collodi	Eugenie Foa	Harry Houidini
C. E. Orr	Eugene Wood	Helent Hunt Jackson
C. M. Ingleby	Evelyn Everett-Green	Helen Nicolay
Carolyn Wells	Everard Cotes	Hendy David Thoreau
Catherine Parr Traill	F. J. Cross	Henrik Ibsen
Charles A. Eastman	Federick Austin Ogg	Henry Adams
Charles Dickens	Ferdinand Ossendowski	Henry Ford
Charles Dudley Warner	Francis Bacon	Henry Frost
Charles Farrar Browne	Francis Darwin	Henry James
Charles Ives	Frances Hodgson Burnett	Henry Jones Ford
Charles Kingsley	Frank Gee Patchin	Henry Seton Merriman
Charles Lathrop Pack	Frank Harris	Henry Wadsworth
Charles Whibley	Frank Jewett Mather	Longfellow
Charles Willing Beale	Frank L. Packard	Henry W Longfellow
Charlotte M. Braeme	Frederick Trevor Hill	Herbert A. Giles
Charlotte M. Yonge	Frederick Winslow Taylor	Herbert N. Casson
Clair W. Hayes	Friedrich Kerst	Herman Hesse
Clarence Day Jr.	Friedrich Nietzsche	Homer
Clarence E. Mulford	Fyodor Dostoyevsky	Honore De Balzac

Horace Walpole
Horatio Alger, Jr.
Howard Pyle
Howard R. Garis
Hugh Lofting
Hugh Walpole
Humphry Ward
Ian Maclaren
Israel Abrahams
J.G.Austin
J. Henri Fabre
J. M. Barrie
J. Macdonald Oxley
J. S. Knowles
J. Storer Clouston
Jack London
Jacob Abbott
James Allen
James Lane Allen
James Andrews
James Baldwin
James DeMille
James Joyce
James Oliver Curwood
James Oppenheim
James Otis
Jane Austen
Jens Peter Jacobsen
Jerome K. Jerome
John Burroughs
John F. Kennedy
John Gay
John Glasworthy
John Habberton
John Joy Bell
John Milton
John Philip Sousa
Jonathan Swift
Joseph Carey
Joseph Conrad
Joseph Jacobs
Julian Hawthrone
Julies Vernes
Justin Huntly McCarthy
Kakuzo Okakura
Kenneth Grahame
Kate Langley Bosher
L. A. Abbot
L. T. Meade
L. Frank Baum
Laura Lee Hope

Laurence Housman
Leo Tolstoy
Leonid Andreyev
Lewis Carroll
Lilian Bell
Lloyd Osbourne
Louis Tracy
Louisa May Alcott
Lucy Fitch Perkins
Lucy Maud Montgomery
Lydia Miller Middleton
Lyndon Orr
M. H. Adams
Margaret E. Sangster
Margaret Vandercook
Maria Edgeworth
Maria Thompson Daviess
Mariano Azuela
Marion Polk Angellotti
Mark Overton
Mark Twain
Mary Austin
Mary Cole
Mary Rowlandson
Mary Wollstonecraft Shelley
Max Beerbohm
Myra Kelly
Nathaniel Hawthrone
O. F. Walton
Oscar Wilde
Owen Johnson
P.G.Wodehouse
Paul and Mable Thorn
Paul G. Tomlinson
Paul Severing
Peter B. Kyne
Plato
R. Derby Holmes
R. L. Stevenson
Rabindranath Tagore
Rahul Alvares
Ralph Waldo Emmerson
Rene Descartes
Rex E. Beach
Richard Harding Davis
Richard Jefferies
Robert Barr
Robert Frost
Robert Gordon Anderson
Robert L. Drake

Robert Lansing
Robert Michael Ballantyne
Robert W. Chambers
Rosa Nouchette Carey
Ross Kay
Rudyard Kipling
Samuel B. Allison
Samuel Hopkins Adams
Sarah Bernhardt
Selma Lagerlof
Sherwood Anderson
Sigmund Freud
Standish O'Grady
Stanley Weyman
Stella Benson
Stephen Crane
Stewart Edward White
Stijn Streuvels
Swami Abhedananda
Swami Parmananda
T. S. Ackland
The Princess Der Ling
Thomas A. Janvier
Thomas A Kempis
Thomas Anderton
Thomas Bailey Aldrich
Thomas Bulfinch
Thomas De Quincey
Thomas H. Huxley
Thomas Hardy
Thomas More
Thornton W. Burgess
U. S. Grant
Valentine Williams
Victor Appleton
Virginia Woolf
Walter Scott
Washington Irving
Wilbur Lawton
Wilkie Collins
Willa Cather
Willard F. Baker
William Makepeace Thackeray
William W. Walter
Winston Churchill
Yei Theodora Ozaki
Young E. Allison
Zane Grey

www.ingramcontent.com/pod-product-compliance
Lightning Source LLC
Chambersburg PA
CBHW020000050426
42450CB00005B/267